1968

be kent

SINGING TECHNIQUE

JOSEPH J. KLEIN

Vocal Scientist,
Instructor,
Lecturer,
Conductor

How to Avoid Vocal Trouble

with
OLE A. SCHJEIDE, Ph.D.
Research Biologist,
Department of Biophysics and Nuclear Medicine,
University of California at Los Angeles

D. VAN NOSTRAND COMPANY, INC.
Princeton, New Jersey, Toronto, London

VAN NOSTRAND REGIONAL OFFICES: *New York, Chicago, San Francisco*

D. VAN NOSTRAND COMPANY, LTD., *London*

D. VAN NOSTRAND COMPANY (Canada), LTD., *Toronto*

Library of Congress Catalog Card No. 67-18071

PRINTED IN THE UNITED STATES OF AMERICA

To my mother and father
Anna and John Kleinsasser

FOREWORD

Since the eighteenth century, many areas of knowledge have been made into sciences through the use of empirical observations followed by arrangement, hypothesis, generalization, and insight. But in some areas, human behavior in particular, data gathering has often proved inadequate for satisfactory generalization. The use of the singing voice is one such area. This book is written to revitalize, some would say "initiate," the scientific method in voice production. To be sure, patience must be exercised by all who would tread so close to the sincere aims and beliefs of good and conscientious voice teachers everywhere, but the rewards are surely worth the effort.

I have studied with Joseph J. Klein, and have known him for a decade and a half. I have been impressed by his relentless pursuit of empirical truth, even when this pursuit led to disappointments and reversals of earlier conclusions. He has used a truly scientific method in a field where few do so. What appears in these pages is distilled from thousands of hours in private lessons, with groups, with physicians, with psychologists, with ever so many singers, and with other teachers. He has achieved almost unbelievable results with the clear schematic way in which he has formulated, modified, and reformulated his vast knowledge so that it could be communicated and understood. Had he done more teaching and less research into the art and science of voice teaching, there might have been more great singers, but the science itself would have been poorer. Actually, eleven of his pupils are now singing leading operatic roles in Europe, in Mexico, in Tokyo; and throughout the United States, one finds many concert-artists and teachers whom he has trained.

It is time that Mr. Klein's memorable findings and insights be presented in book form. I believe the entire singing profession will be the richer.

John W. Carson, Ph.D.
Chairman, Department of History
Midwestern University
Wichita Falls, Texas

ACKNOWLEDGMENTS

The author would like to express his gratitude for the considerable assistance, direct and indirect, of a large number of individuals in the fields of anatomy, physiology, psychology, and the physics of sound. Among these are:

Mr. Wilmer T. Bartholomew, Dr. Carl Bishop, Dr. Harry Gilbert, Dr. LeRoy Harvey, Dr. Orrie E. Ghrist, Dr. Chevalier Jackson, Dr. Paul J. Moses, Dr. Floyd S. Muckey, Mr. Arnold Rose, Dr. Douglas Stanley, Dr. David P. Unruh, Mr. William Vennard, Mr. John C. Wilcox, Dr. Sam Wilson.

He also wishes to gratefully acknowledge permission granted by CIBA for the use of colored plates from "The Larynx" by Drs. William H. Saunders, Frank H. Netter, and J. Harold Walton; also to The Bell Telephone Co. for high speed action photographs of the vocal cords; and to The American Academy of Teachers of Singing for permission to use portions of their article "Choral Singing and The Responsibility of the Choral Director", through the courtesy of Harold C. Luckstone, Secretary.

CONTENTS

THE HUMAN VOICE IS THE ORGAN OF THE SOUL

—Longfellow

introduction

BIRDS SING BUT CANNOT
PLAY INSTRUMENTS

Now and again out of every generation there bursts upon the singing scene a great natural voice. These voices are like gifts from God but for most people, singing is an acquired art. Possessors of great natural voices provide the example of what is meant by the title of this introduction. Singing correctly by innate instinct, they are very much like birds—they sing but they have no idea how.

Because they are totally unaware of the anatomy of voice or of the basic principles that underlie their every tone, as they grow older and their habits change, their muscles become weaker and they tend to lose their voices. This can occur gradually or abruptly, but it occurs all too often.

More fortunate in many respects is the singer who is perhaps a bit less vocally coordinated by nature, but who, by chance or by plan, comes into contact with a teacher sufficiently enlightened to have examined the art of singing from an objective, if not detached, perspective. Assuming that the study has been thoroughly carried out, that there are no conflicting factors in the methodology, and that an awareness of what really constitutes the ideal voice exists, such a teacher or school can theoretically mold the voice of almost any musically endowed individual to match or exceed the range, the quality, and the volume ever found in any so-called natural voice. What is more, if this trained voice is maintained along the same principles by which it was developed, it should last a lifetime.

After all, the natural singer has only standard equipment. He stands apart from other individuals chiefly because of an innate natural coordination (largely due to freedom from interference by muscles that are intended for purposes other than singing). It is the function of the vocal scientist to seek out impartially and correctly, the parameters which permit such coordination to exist; and it is the function of the vocal teacher to utilize this knowledge in the maintenance of natural voices and in the construction of new ones.

There are, however, some major problems facing less-gifted aspirants, the least of which is talent. First, the right teacher or the right school must be found. All teachers and all schools are not equal. Many a teacher is teaching voice because he has lost his own. This is not necessarily an adverse criticism because the shock of his experience may have served as the stimulus for a profound study of the problem. Eventually, he may have gained considerable insight. However, many of these teachers are equipped only to listen, not to remedy or to train. One of the ways in which the prospective candidate might choose a studio is to examine the product. If he likes the voices developed there, he may have a legitimate reason for beginning his training in that school. Before committing himself, he should also try to learn by reading as much as he possibly can about what voice is or what it should be.

Usually, in contrast to the natural singer, the great trained artist is an intellectual, or is under the constant guidance of an analytical person. In addition, he must have tremendous motivation and drive. This is necessary to overcome the second great drawback which is the prodigious amount of energy and time that must be invested for an acceptable return. Again, in contrast to the natural voice, the singer who has not been blessed with this gift must often unlearn bad habits before he can begin learning good ones. This may take months or years. Development of a new voice is a gradual process with a few steep climbs and many seemingly endless plateaus. Unless he is very careful, he should refrain from exhibition singing during most of the training period. Plain boredom has caused many singers to abandon such a regimen, and thus lose all chances of attaining the real goal. Although Enrico Caruso was endowed with great natural singing ability, history reveals that he spent a number of years developing his superb instrument before introducing it to an eventually adoring public.[1] To most individuals even great success is not worth the effort.

Although many famous singers of the past were in this sense accidents, it was a still greater accident if they remained vocally great for any length of time. Singers have for centuries been subjected to the opinions of those who, having no sound basis for their opinions, were eager to give them, nonetheless. Following a given performance the same singer has been said to be wonderful by some and very bad by others. Allowing some latitude for personal taste, could both have been right? If worthless judgment only serves to confuse the music-loving public, it is bad enough, but unfortunately, it does not stop there. Many careers are ruined each year by chance criticism in the form of approval as well as disapproval.

Over sixty years ago Dr. Floyd Muckey[2] wrote: "Voice criticism today is not real criticism, but merely praise or censure. It does not aid the performer to improve his production or educate the public to appreciate the difference between good and bad voices. It leaves the singer and the speaker at the mercy of the mood of the critic. If a critic were required to give reasons for his statements, he would be much more careful in expressing his opinion."

Much is heard of the "Golden Age of Singing." The mystery of when this period flourished is as great as the ignorance of the music critics and vocal teachers of years gone by about what constitutes correct and incorrect singing. The simple fact is that no sound basis for a judgment or criticism of voice could exist (with respect to either esthetic values or physiological correctness) until vocal scientists accomplished for the vocal profession what medical and other scientific researchers have done for the health and well being of the human body. Investigators of vocal phenomena have looked first at the physical laws that govern the emission, transmittance, and perception of sound; they have reviewed the roles of the various anatomical structures in the making of sound and the physiological factors which must be exploited if one is to produce correct and reproducible sounds. Such investigations were initiated and, indeed, carried out to a remarkable extent over fifty years ago by pioneers, such as Muckey and Hallock.[3] Most of the information published by these men is as valid today as it was then. However, the line of communication between vocal scientists and practicing teachers is not always open, with the result that much of the data gathered by these early workers dwindled into obscurity before it could come to the attention of these who would have benefited from it most.

Since the early years, much additional data has been assembled concerning the vocal apparatus and the nature of the voice. Examination of musical periodicals published during the last decade reveals a considerable expansion of interest in scientific aspects of voice production and some of the older findings have been rediscovered more than once.

The author does not feel that he has made more than small contributions to the large bulk of scientific knowledge, for no one man can hope to arrive at many answers via the tedious laboratory route. His major role has been that of accumulator, sifter, and finally, practitioner, on the basis of the considerable body of investigative data that has come to light during the past half-century. The present book is the fruit of twenty-five years devoted to this pursuit. He considers himself extremely fortunate to have lived at the very point in history when so many scientific advances have been forthcoming, including revolutionary findings in the science of voice.

As this book will seek to demonstrate, sufficient understanding is now available so that an "ideal" voice can both be created and be intelligently appreciated. Recently a great singer, Marilyn Horne,[4] has met with an ecstatic reception from critics and public alike. Miss Horne has an extensive range, formidable reserves of power, and exhibits no abrupt changes in quality from one tone to another. While perhaps there will never be a "perfect" voice (due to physical limitations), at this writing Marilyn Horne presents a phenomenal example of the vocal coordination that voice scientists are striving to instill in every singer. Except for slight shrillness occasionally on a very high pitch, Miss Horne's voice on the record "Presenting Marilyn Horne" (London Label) can serve as a blueprint for the "ideal" hereafter referred to in this volume.

It should be emphasized that proper development of the voices of high school and college students, especially those who have done relatively little singing, is much easier than the training of individuals who have had much more singing experience. After introducing a few fundamental concepts, all that is required to obtain basi-

cally correct vocal production is a careful ear and enough
time for the voice to mature. It is largely for these young
people that this book has been written. The author does
not expect students to pick it up and absorb its message
without other help, but the teachers of these young people
will certainly be able to appreciate the principles outlined
herein, and if their students are trained accordingly, considerable time and heartbreak will be spared them.

Armed with the available information and employing the proper technique, the vocal instructor can now
take almost any untrained young person and develop a
voice with an even vocal line, more than adequate
power, and pleasing quality throughout a range of three
octaves. Reconstruction of an injured voice is more difficult, not only because the individual obviously must unlearn bad habits but also because certain muscles, liga-
ments, and cartilages have become altered due to misuse.
The age of the individual is a factor here, but if the singer
is willing to invest a prodigious amount of time and energy, the voice can usually be regained and sometimes
improved over the original product. The author has
worked with several singers with broken voices, and they
have eventually attained ranges of three octaves in a perfect singing line. These, he feels, provide the evidence
that a real breakthrough has been made in the school of
voice production. Most of the facts, principles, and exercises which resulted in these achievements are outlined in
this book, ready for exploitation by vocal teachers, choir
directors, and students. Although there is still much to be
done in the vocal laboratory, the aspiring singer need no

longer start from scratch. A sufficiently solid foundation has been laid so that with hard work, persistence, and an attentive ear, the desired result is within every singer's grasp.

This book is not intended as an all-embracing text. It emphasizes the instructive aspects of vocal training and defines the reasons behind this plan of instruction. It is purposely written in layman's language so that it can be understood by a wide range of readers. It is the author's hope that it will be read by teachers so that it can serve as a basis for the instruction of singers according to laboratory-proved principles; by students so that they can develop for themselves the concepts which will guide their singing; by those who have speech problems so that they can be inspired to correct their difficulties; and by critics and the general public to help them acquire new understanding of this important cultural area.

chapter one
SUPPORT

THE IMPORTANCE OF SUPPORT

Breathing is as normal for human beings as is running.[5] A runner must, however, learn to move his legs in an extraordinary fashion if he is to become a champion, and the same is true of breathing for the outstanding vocal artist. The great singer is an extraordinarily skilled breather.[6] The reason is that only the respiratory muscles, properly employed, can fully and correctly provide SUPPORT, and *Support is basic to all parameters of good voice production.*

Many singers are uncertain what constitutes Support; it is, in fact, nothing more nor less than a physiological act. It is the controlled interaction of the two opposing sets of breathing muscles in passing air between the vocal cords and in closing the glottis by controlling the arytenoid cartilages (Fig. 1 and Color Plate I), so that air does not escape unused and so that the muscles within the cords can—with minimal interference, and thus consistently—adjust to the tensions necessary to produce the desired speeds of vibration. Failure to understand the full nature and importance of Support, with resulting lack of application, is to blame for a major part of the confusion that has prevailed in the profession since the beginning of the School of Voice.

As previously mentioned, Support is provided by the breathing muscles. Four groups are involved. Two of these control inhalation:

(1) The diaphragm (affords most of resistance for Support)

(2) The intercostal muscles that pull the ribs outward

Two other groups control exhalation:

(3) The abdominal muscles (exert the upward thrust against the diaphragm)

(4) The intercostal muscles that pull the ribs inward.

Ordinarily, these sets of muscles of contrasting motion do not oppose each other strongly. The set governing inhalation tenses and then relaxes as the opposing set tenses for exhalation. However, if these two sets of muscles are applied *against each other* so as to produce a *continuous* state of tension during the act of measured exhalation, the glottis (Fig. 1) can be firmly closed and kept in a closed position—a condition which shall soon be perceived by the reader as being unique and imperative to good tone production. The physiological basis for the closing of the glottis by this means is as follows: When the inhalation muscles (which pull the diaphragm down and the ribs outward) and the exhalation muscles (which pull the abdominal muscles upward and the ribs inward) are exerted at the same time, the colliding action whips the arytenoid cartilages into action by reflex (closure of the glottis by this means is the body's mechanism for creating intra-thoracic pressure—see the diagram of the action of the arytenoid cartilages shown in Color Plate I— thus closing the glottis and bringing the vocal cords close together. This is what occurs when an individual barks like a dog. However, the condition in a bark is extremely transitory because the opposition of the two sets of muscles is immediately released once the bark has been emitted. The correct staccato sound is produced by identical physiological means. Continued application of Support under these conditions produces a sustained bark (or howl). In order to sustain the opposition of the breathing muscles, resistance must be afforded by the inhalation muscles, and slightly overmatching force must be exerted by the muscles governing exhalation. A popular theory holds that the Bernoulli effect assists in "sucking" the vocal folds together as air is passing between them.[6] This

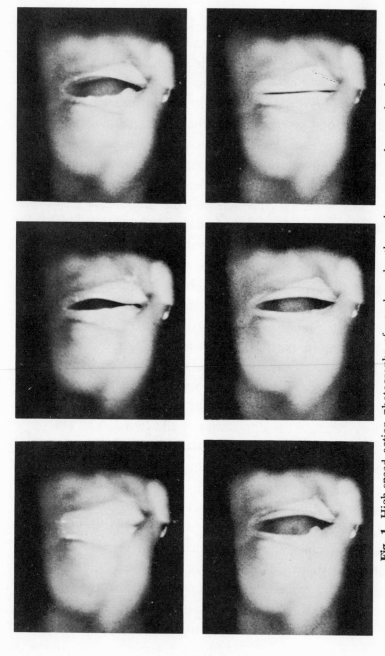

Fig. 1. High-speed action photographs of vocal cords: through one complete cycle of vibration at a frequency of about 125 cycles per second, or approximately an octave below middle C. *Courtesy of Bell Telephone Laboratories Incorporated.*

seems unlikely because the small amount of air passing in puffs between the cords does not create enough force to cause this much suction, especially in view of the thinness of the vibrating edges of the folds.

It may be useful at this point for the reader to perform a few barks, howls, and staccatos in order to experience, in an exaggerated fashion, the feeling of Support. Even after experiencing this feeling (especially if this is the first time), the reader may be reluctant to accept the premise that this is the proper way to close the glottis, and hence the proper way to sing correctly. In his earlier training he may have been told, "put the tone up," "place it forward," "put it on the teeth," or "get it into the nose." [7] From such bad advice he may have learned that the swallowing muscles may also close the glottis. These muscles come into play when one applies slight pressure to the jaw and raises the larynx up against the hyoid bone (Figs. 2a and 2c) as a result of pushing the tongue against the roof of the mouth. Pressing the lips together also tends to close the glottis, tightens the ventricular bands, and depresses the epiglottis.

Using the swallowing muscles for closing the glottis, singing or speaking is categorically wrong! A consistent mode of closure of the glottis must be achieved so that the vocal cords are in exactly the same relative position or state of freedom (and the surrounding musculature is uniformly set) each time they are called upon to tense for a given pitch. No closure by the swallowing muscles is either sufficient or consistent. Even more destructive, both immediately and with respect to any hopes the singer

may have for the future, is the fact that employment of
the swallowing muscles counteracts the correct muscular
applications that are being made for the production of
sound. When the glottis is closed incorrectly, by means

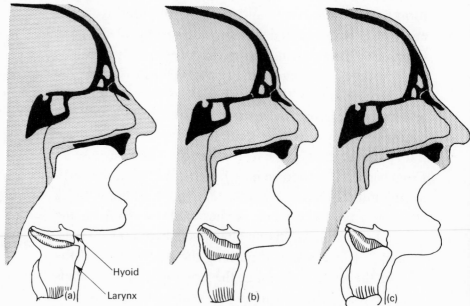

Fig. 2. a. WRONG. Larynx is down, but the hyoid bone is also down
and pressing against it. **b.** CORRECT. Larynx is freely down, hyoid bone
up. Ample space between the two. **c.** WRONG. Hyoid bone is in correct position, but larynx has been drawn up against it due to contraction
of the swallowing muscles.

of the swallowing muscles, the larynx shifts upward and
presses against the hyoid bone (Fig. 2c), the jaw stiffens,
and the position and lack of flexibility of the tongue is
such that it becomes impossible for the singer to make the
proper adjustments for resonance and vowel formation.

The resulting tones are dull, scratchy, and, of course, incorrect.

More often than not, as he begins a phrase, a singer will produce two or three tones using the breathing apparatus (Support) as the sole means of closing the glottis. This is usually a relatively unconscious act which takes place because it is the most natural means of producing tones. However, upon attempting notes higher on the scale, the singer usually fails to make the proper adjustments of the resonance chambers; then sensing that something is wrong, he will bring into play increasing numbers of interfering muscles, including the swallowing muscles. The immediate result is vocal disaster, although the uneducated ear may not always recognize it as such. More important, insidious physical damage is inflicted when the singer overindulges in this improper practice. Examination of the singing equipment of an individual who has utilized the swallowing muscles for closure of the glottis over a period of time reveals that the larynx will set itself hard against the hyoid bone (Fig. 2c), sometimes even before the singer begins to sing. Manipulation of the larynx shows it to be grossly inflexible, held rigidly by muscles that go into spasm at the slightest provocation. The muscles at the root of the tongue and the mylohyoid are also under involuntary tension when the larynx is low (Fig. 2a).

Many muscles are involved in the correct production of sound. Those that initiate Support (the breathing muscles) and those of the tongue are under voluntary control, but many are involuntary. For example, when voluntary collision of the breathing muscles is effected, it is almost impossible to stop the reflex action resulting in the closure of the glottis. At the same time the ventricular bands must keep the laryngeal box from collapsing. These muscles are representative of the countless muscles not under direct control, but which are weak and inconsistent in the neophyte singer. They must be strengthened and molded more firmly into a coordinated, conditioned reflex by constantly using correct voice production.

INTERFERING MUSCLES

The muscles that interfere with voice production are initially all voluntary. However, persistence of bad habits leads to the establishment of badly conditioned reflexes so that, under the stimulus of having to sing, the performer automatically brings into play not only the wrong voluntary muscles but also a host of involuntary muscles that perform by habit in a pattern that is detrimental to free vocal production.

Swallowing muscles have already been implicated as interfering muscles. It should be emphasized that mastery of correct Support leaves the singer free of the temptation to employ them. Another important group of muscles which can interfere with Support are certain muscles of the abdomen—those which enable a mother to deliver a child and, hence, pull downward. The student should learn to distinguish particularly between the transverse and oblique abdominal muscles which provide Support and those which pull downward. When the *lower* abdominal muscles are exerted during song, the effect on Support is analagous to applying the emergency brake on a car. All the components of the singing track are jerked out of place and that critical center, the larynx, is sent into spasm. In practicing Support, the student must keep in mind that when a capacity breath is taken, the diaphragm is already at its *lowest* position (Fig. 3a). Any force against it must come from below, pressing upward (Figs. 3b, c, and d). Note that in *abdominal* breathing (Fig. 3d) the position of the stomach is contrary to its position in *rib* breathing (when the stomach is drawn in while taking a breath). Correct Support is like holding the breath and trying to exhale at the same time, that is, the opposing sets of breathing muscles (in and out) are exerted at the same time.

Still another caution must be administered regarding interference with Support. This is the tendency of the student in his preparation for the act of singing, to assume an exaggerated upright stance or "swayback" position (Fig. 4a). This restricts the upward pull of the abdominal muscles necessary for correct Support. Actually, the beginning student need not stand while vocalizing. He should sit on a stool and adjust his lower back against a wall or piano in such a fashion that the usual "swayback" posture (Fig. 4a) is absolutely corrected (Fig. 4b). With the back straight and the lower abdominal muscles relaxed, the subject can now exert the upward pull for correct Support. However, the shoulders should not be thrust unnaturally backward; in fact, a slight rounding of the back

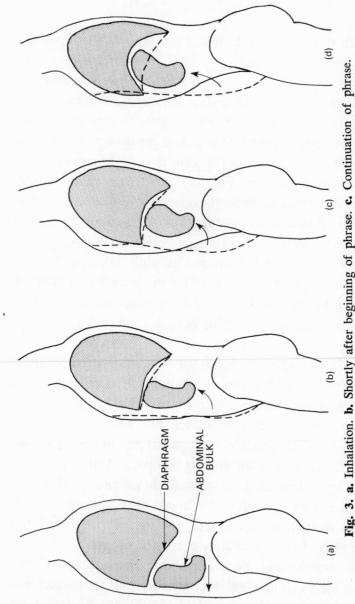

Fig. 3. a. Inhalation. **b.** Shortly after beginning of phrase. **c.** Continuation of phrase. **d.** End of phrase. Dotted lines in **b, c,** and **d** represent original positions of chest, belly, and diaphragm.

DIAPHRAGM

ABDOMINAL
BULK

(a) (b) (c) (d)

is permissible. Later, when the correct posture has been repeatedly experienced in this fashion, the student may sing while standing, attempting to maintain the identical posture that he has become familiar with in the sitting

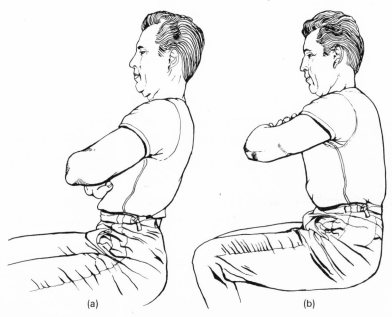

(a)   (b)

Fig. 4. a. WRONG. Subject is in "swayback" position. **b.** CORRECT. Subject's back is straight.

position. If the singer finds that he can, without undue tension, correct his naturally occurring "swayback" posture, he is well on his way toward the attainment of Support. In this stance, there is a minimal possibility of creating uneven tensions that might be reflected in the intercostal muscles, especially those that supplement the resistance afforded by the diaphragm.

DEVELOPMENT OF SUPPORT

Once the student has accepted the concept of opposition of the breathing muscles (that is, Support) as the only reliable means of properly closing the glottis and thus adjusting the larynx and the vocal cords, he is ready to proceed with the development of Support.

The statement is often made that speaking and singing are synonymous. While partly true, this idea has led to a great deal of confusion. Speaking is the simple utterance of sound complimented by vowels and consonants in a manner to make oneself understood by one's fellowman. It is not normally necessary to sustain a given word or sound over a long period of time or to produce it on any particular pitch. The act of speech is, therefore, performed in the most comfortable part of one's voice where a minimum of effort is required. Singing is quite different. A quality of sound is desired which is of smooth transition from pure pitch to pure pitch and is of considerable range and intensity. This must be produced under conditions in which the pitch and length of phrase have been predetermined by the composer. To say to the singer, "sing as you speak" is an insidious understatement and is wrong because it completely ignores the concept of Support. One can say to a singer "sing as you speak" *only* when speech is completely correct; and still he must be taught to sustain the vocal sound.

In the old school of fencing, the neophyte is shown the proper movements, and then is made to practice these day after day until the movements become absolutely automatic. He is not allowed even to practice with an opponent until muscle memory is perfectly instilled, although this may take several years. Yet, the beginning fencer is usually in a better position to learn to fence than the singer is to learn to sing because all the fencer has to do is to learn. The contemporary singer, however, must nearly always *un*learn the bad habits carried over from speech and incorrect voice production before he can begin to learn. The section of this chapter "Understanding Support" (page 26) is primarily for the use of teachers who find that certain of their students have particular difficulty in unlearning bad singing habits.

Since the potential singer must begin somewhere to develop Support, he may as well do so in bed. Upon waking in the quiet of the morning, he should first observe how the breathing muscles function. Although in the horizontal position, the chest remains relatively motionless; the abdominal muscles just below the sternum move vertically up and down. The downward movement creates pressure against the diaphragm, which has already been referred to as one of the primary muscles involved in exhalation. An experiment may now be carried out to determine how even more pressure can be exerted against the diaphragm for the production of sound: Without previously taking an extraordinarily deep breath, the student should continue one of the exhalations to a great extreme by blowing out all the air he can. This exercise will bring into play those abdominal muscles that form the basis for Support. Since the lower abdominal muscles are automatically relaxed when the subject is lying flat, the student can readily exert the leverage of the *transverse* and *oblique muscles* in such a way that they raise the belly upward against the stomach, liver, and spleen, causing these organs to press forcibly but smoothly against the diaphragm (Figs. 5b, c, and d). While still lying in bed, the student should attempt to vocalize softly, using these muscles to aid exhalation. In subsequent attempts at Support, when the student becomes aware that any other muscles (except the inhalation muscles that are automatically affording resistance) are in a state of tension, he must immediately seek to relax these because they only encumber the intended exercise.

After the student has experienced Support of a more or less passive nature, as that described above, he is ready to proceed with a more vigorous application. This may be carried out while sitting or standing. It consists of a positive rolling motion of the abdominal muscles. Beginning with a pushing out of the abdomen just below the level of the navel (Fig. 3a), this same region is firmly depressed inward and is then lifted upward until pressure against the diaphragm is strongly felt (Figs. 3b, c, and d). Of course, the pressure is not effective unless some resistance is afforded by the diaphragm, but resistance is an automatic reflex action if the rolling exercise is carried out correctly. Repetition of this rolling movement many times in succession, three or four times a day, without breathing or forming a sound, is a splendid exercise for the development of the muscles employed in Support.

Other exercises that should aid in the development of these muscles include:

1) While lying flat on the floor, bring the knees up so that the back of the heels touch the buttocks (Fig. 5). This exercise strengthens exhalation muscles. Repeat it several times and follow it immediately with several successive abdominal muscle-rolling exercises as described in the preceding paragraph.

Fig. 5. Exercise for strengthening exhalation muscles.

2) While lying on the floor, knees bent, place the insteps under some solid object, such as a radiator, and with hands at sides or clasped behind the head, elevate and lower the body several times (Fig. 6). Follow immediately with the abdominal-rolling exercise, upright. This exercise should be done at least six times daily to start, and the number of exercises should be increased gradually.

3) While lying flat with hands clasped behind the head, lift the legs (keeping the knees straight) until the feet are twenty-four inches above the floor or about a forty-five degree angle. Keeping the lower back flat against

the floor, lower the legs slowly to within six inches of the floor and raise again (Figs. 7a and b). This exercise should be done two to three times daily to start. It can

Fig. 6. Subject raises body up and down to develop abdominal muscles.

be discontinued as the stomach muscles become better conditioned. Repeat the exercise several times before stopping to carry out the abdominal-rolling exercise, upright.

In addition to faithfully performing the above exercises, the student should:

1) Be mentally aware of what Support is, and think about it continuously.

2) Experience the feeling of smoothly applied Support without vocalizing whenever he has a moment to spare.

3) Vocalize by means of Support alone, assuming the correct posture and relaxed state. In this case lower the diaphragm as far as possible for capacity breath and

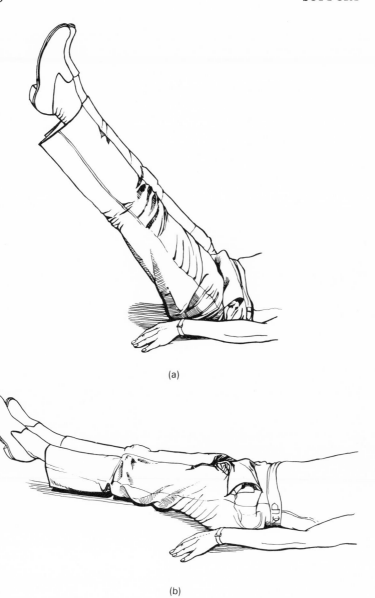

(a)

(b)

Fig. 7. a. Legs are up at a forty-five degree angle. Knees are straight.
b. Subject brings legs down to within six inches of the floor and then
raises them back up.

retain this tension (i.e. hold your breath) through the attack, which is accomplished by a gradual upward thrust on the part of the abdominal muscles.

4) Keep a sharp lookout for signs of interference from other muscles.

5) Seek the assistance of a teacher who is familiar with these concepts and regularly check for faults.

6) Avoid singing songs until muscle memory is well established.

7) Eat and sleep properly—exercise until a state of relaxation is achieved.

8) Not despair—not give up!

As in all great skills, muscular and mental, the attainment of Support will only gradually become an automatic reflex action. Once the proper coordination has been worked out, the singer will perceive that Support is not a mighty force, not a means of creating great pressure, but is rather a source of confident power underlying all that is necessary for a controlled singing line. The student should remember that the entire "sound track" is built around this shaft, and if it is shaped straight and strong, other elements will fall into place. Without Support, concern with further components of voice is pointless.

UNDERSTANDING SUPPORT

Understanding correct Support is a matter of using the proper muscles and nearly every human being has these in adequate numbers and in potential strength. How-

ever, the singer who uses incorrect physical forces to produce sound is helpless to do anything different until the
correct coordinations are induced. Perhaps reading a book
such as this one will be sufficient to steer many errant
singers in the right direction. Sometimes, however, incorrect voice production employed over a period of time will
have become such a habit that the pupil must literally be
"shaken" from his existing plight. This can best be done
by "honest deception." W. T. Bartholomew writes:

> . . . in teaching voice, circumlocution is necessary.
> The required setting must be secured through round-
> about and subtle ways. The throat must be coaxed
> or surprised into its proper shape, until a measure
> of control be gained. The teacher who attempts to
> teach singing, an accoustical and physiological phe-
> nomenon, purely by the aid of imagery, without
> understanding accoustical and physiological princi-
> ples himself, is surely at a disadvantage.[8]

Therefore, the student must be fooled in order to fool his
"built in" incorrect coordination. His old approach to
making sounds will always bring the same bad reflexes
into action.

The nerve centers that effect the closure of the glottis following stimulation by the breathing muscles must
be activated. This center is in the area of the solar plexus.
When it is activated, the glottis closes smoothly by reflex,
the cords are free to vibrate and muscles prone to interfere with the position of the larynx and the movement of
the tongue are relatively relaxed. Until then, nothing is

right. (The competent vocal instructor will know when this phenomenon has taken place. If he does not know, he is helpless to bring about any positive change.) The induction of such activation is the most difficult of all phases of voice production. The nerve center can only be properly energized by opposition of the inhalation and exhalation muscles of the breathing apparatus. At this point the student may have become discouraged. However, neither he nor especially his teacher should give up easily. The reward is too great.

The teacher actually has a choice of several ways of activating the reflex that closes the glottis. One is to alert the breathing muscles by fast panting, breathing out until only little air remains. The chest should be held rather high with no sound being uttered. In some cases, having the student produce the correct staccato sound, as previously mentioned, is very helpful. Another, slightly more drastic procedure, is to have the student bark like a dog, not making sounds that are necessarily beautiful or on any particular pitch, but engendering quick attacks that strike the two groups of breathing muscles against each other like the collision of two moving objects coming from opposite directions. The danger of persisting interference by muscles in the jaw and in the lower abdomen is, however, still present, and these areas should be closely watched by the instructor.

Perhaps the fastest way in which to engender the free sound for a singer who cannot be reached by the aforementioned technique is to have him lie flat on his back. When the body is in a horizontal position, those muscles which are necessarily tensed to sustain it in an upright position immediately relax. Now the abdominal part of the body becomes somewhat like a hot water bottle. If one presses on one end, the water moves to the other end. The singer does not need to fight the law of gravity while moving the components of his belly toward his chest. He can more easily supply correct Support by

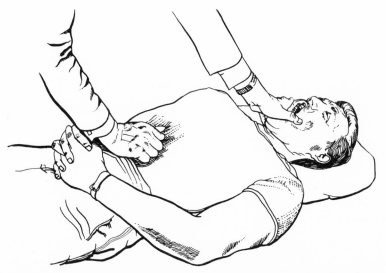

Fig. 8. Subject and instructor working to activate the reflex that closes the glottis.

placing his folded hands on the lower part of the abdomen and pulling upward (Fig. 8). This moves the necessary bulk up under the diaphragm.

There is, moreover, another great advantage inherent in this procedure. Since an abnormal reaction in an abnormal situation is normal behavior, a strong psychological weapon is brought to bear on the problem. Incorrect vocal production employed over a period of time has become normal. An abnormal reaction is now called for from this singer, hence the abnormal situation.

With the student still in the horizontal position, the mentor can bring about an amazing result by placing the heel of his hand about four inches below the sternum and vibrating his hand up and down at the rate of about four or five vibrations per second while the singer makes a sound on almost any pitch in the early range of his voice. If this does not result in an immediate free sound, it is possible that the fault is a stiff jaw. The teacher can repeat the process, this time placing his other hand on the singer's jaw, making sure that his subject is completely relaxed (Fig. 8). Teacher and student should work in this manner until the desired effect is obtained.

However, if results are not forthcoming in five to ten efforts, the teacher should stop and check to see if the larynx and the hyoid bone are separating at the point of inhalation (Fig. 2b). If so, the finger and thumb should be kept there for the next attack to observe if this space snaps shut for the attack. This space must remain separated as it is when inhaling. However, when a case is severe, in order to help break the bad reflex, it is necessary to hold the larynx and hyoid bone apart with fingers and thumb. (In a very bad case of rigid larynx, the space between the hyoid bone and the larynx never opens, not even for breathing.)

Once the singer has experienced a really free and resonant sound, he is never satisfied with anything less. To him it is like a light suddenly turned on in the darkness. The teacher's first great victory is won because from now on he has the student's complete cooperation. At this point use the tongue exercise (Chapter 2, page 51). The singer has now moved into a new realm of thinking. His power of concentration will become a source of strength. To accomplish what the teacher has helped him to experience, the sound he created with his own voice, even though he needs assistance, gives him a definite objective to concentrate upon, and his power of concentration increases in the process.

TREATING A SPEECH PROBLEM— A CASE HISTORY

Recently a young man, typical of many who have been referred to this studio, presented himself for analysis and treatment. This man is a teacher in a college, and his position demands that he lecture as much as six hours a day. During the past year his voice had become progressively worse and by the end of the school year he had practically lost it altogether. His physician said that he was no longer using his vocal cords (folds), and perhaps was achieving a measure of speech by contraction of the ventricular bands (which is the manner in which speech is achieved by a person who has temporarily lost control of the adductor action of the vocal cords). The ventricular bands lie a short distance above the vocal cords but are certainly not intended to be used as origins of sound (Fig. 9a).

Naturally, this young man was desperate when he arrived at the studio, and he volunteered to follow instruction to the letter (for a year, if need be) if only he could regain the faculty of speech. He was assured that the cure would not be so long in coming.

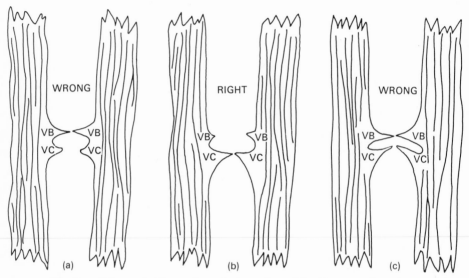

Fig. 9. a. Schematic illustration of phonation with either vocal cords or ventricular bands. VB = Ventricular Bands. VC = Vocal Cords. Diagram **b** shows correct phonation. The situation depicted in **c** can create a dual pitch.

Examination of the larynx revealed that it was typically inflexible and was pressed hard against the hyoid bone (Fig. 2c). Some time was therefore spent in manipulation of this organ as described in Chapter 3, page 53, paragraph 3. When the larynx had relaxed somewhat, he was placed in a horizontal position to make sounds and alternate treatments were undertaken, including (1) manual vibration of the solar plexus (the region a few inches

below the sternum) and (2) activation of the belly inward
and upward toward the chest (Fig. 9). The sounds first
engendered were very strange to him. This was because
they were created by a completely foreign muscular coordination. However, after a few of these treatments, he
was able, by employment of the breathing muscles, to
activate the adductor muscles of the vocal cords, thus
producing creditable sounds on his own. Because his
muscular coordination required a complete overhauling,
he was sent home with the following instructions: For at
least one eight-hour period he was to make the new sounds
in the proper way for five minutes every quarter hour,
each time resting ten minutes. By the time he had done
this, some muscular memory had been established. After
this start, he solved the remainder of his problem easily.

chapter two
RESONANCE

This chapter is primarily concerned with pitch and resonance. Pitch is initiated by the vocal cords. The major resonators which affect the pitch are the pharynxes and nasal cavities. The moveable parts for adjusting these instruments are the tongue and the soft palate.

PITCH

Although a tone of a given pitch can be produced in a number of different ways, the pitch elicited from all instruments is a function of a number of pulsations of air occurring per unit time. The fundamental pitch of a voiced sound is based on the number of puffs of air waves per

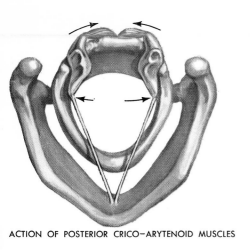

ACTION OF POSTERIOR CRICO–ARYTENOID MUSCLES

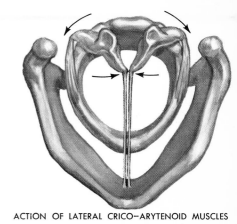

ACTION OF LATERAL CRICO–ARYTENOID MUSCLES

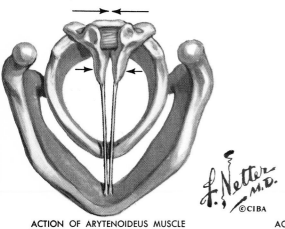

ACTION OF ARYTENOIDEUS MUSCLE

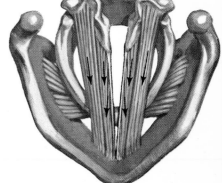

ACTION OF VOCALIS AND THYRO–ARYTENOID MUSCLES

Plate I. Action of Arytenoideus.

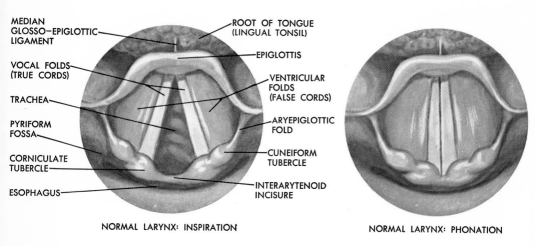

MEDIAN GLOSSO-EPIGLOTTIC LIGAMENT

VOCAL FOLDS (TRUE CORDS)

TRACHEA

PYRIFORM FOSSA

CORNICULATE TUBERCLE

ESOPHAGUS

ROOT OF TONGUE (LINGUAL TONSIL)

EPIGLOTTIS

VENTRICULAR FOLDS (FALSE CORDS)

ARYEPIGLOTTIC FOLD

CUNEIFORM TUBERCLE

INTERARYTENOID INCISURE

NORMAL LARYNX: INSPIRATION

a

NORMAL LARYNX: PHONATION

b

Plate II. a. Vocal cords at rest during inhalation. **b.** Vocal cords are closed. With no opening there is no sound. Fig. 1 illustrates the small opening required for sound.

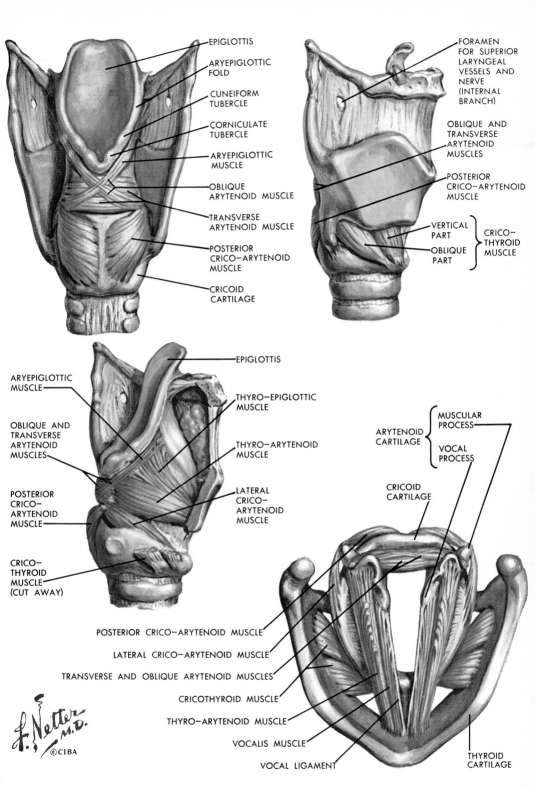

EPIGLOTTIS

ARYEPIGLOTTIC
FOLD

CUNEIFORM
TUBERCLE

CORNICULATE
TUBERCLE

ARYEPIGLOTTIC
MUSCLE

OBLIQUE
ARYTENOID MUSCLE

TRANSVERSE
ARYTENOID MUSCLE

POSTERIOR
CRICO–ARYTENOID
MUSCLE

CRICOID
CARTILAGE

FORAMEN
FOR SUPERIOR
LARYNGEAL
VESSELS AND
NERVE
(INTERNAL
BRANCH)

OBLIQUE AND
TRANSVERSE
ARYTENOID
MUSCLES

POSTERIOR
CRICO–ARYTENOID
MUSCLE

VERTICAL
PART

OBLIQUE
PART

CRICO–
THYROID
MUSCLE

ARYEPIGLOTTIC
MUSCLE

OBLIQUE AND
TRANSVERSE
ARYTENOID
MUSCLES

POSTERIOR
CRICO–
ARYTENOID
MUSCLE

CRICO–
THYROID
MUSCLE
(CUT AWAY)

EPIGLOTTIS

THYRO–EPIGLOTTIC
MUSCLE

THYRO–ARYTENOID
MUSCLE

LATERAL
CRICO–
ARYTENOID
MUSCLE

MUSCULAR
PROCESS

ARYTENOID
CARTILAGE

VOCAL
PROCESS

CRICOID
CARTILAGE

POSTERIOR CRICO–ARYTENOID MUSCLE

LATERAL CRICO–ARYTENOID MUSCLE

TRANSVERSE AND OBLIQUE ARYTENOID MUSCLES

CRICOTHYROID MUSCLE

THYRO–ARYTENOID MUSCLE

VOCALIS MUSCLE

VOCAL LIGAMENT

THYROID
CARTILAGE

Plate III. Intrinsic muscles of the larynx.

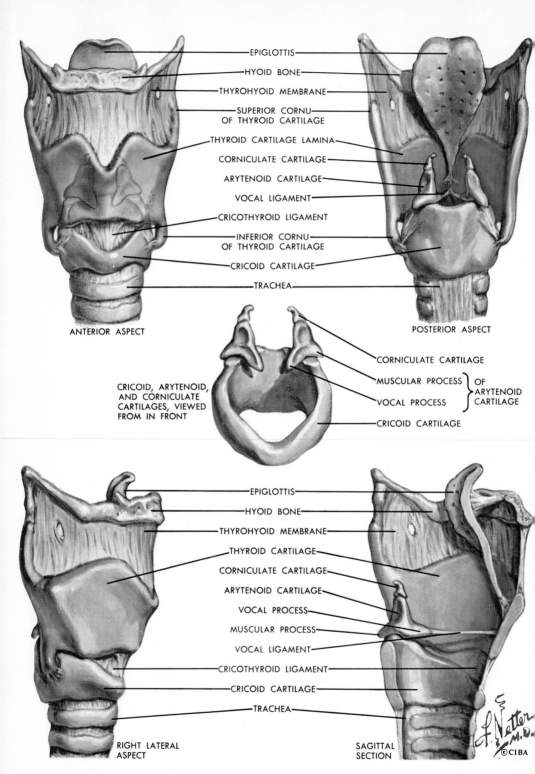

EPIGLOTTIS
HYOID BONE
THYROHYOID MEMBRANE
SUPERIOR CORNU OF THYROID CARTILAGE
THYROID CARTILAGE LAMINA
CORNICULATE CARTILAGE
ARYTENOID CARTILAGE
VOCAL LIGAMENT
CRICOTHYROID LIGAMENT
INFERIOR CORNU OF THYROID CARTILAGE
CRICOID CARTILAGE
TRACHEA

ANTERIOR ASPECT

POSTERIOR ASPECT

CRICOID, ARYTENOID, AND CORNICULATE CARTILAGES, VIEWED FROM IN FRONT

CORNICULATE CARTILAGE
MUSCULAR PROCESS ⎫
VOCAL PROCESS ⎬ OF ARYTENOID CARTILAGE
CRICOID CARTILAGE

EPIGLOTTIS
HYOID BONE
THYROHYOID MEMBRANE
THYROID CARTILAGE
CORNICULATE CARTILAGE
ARYTENOID CARTILAGE
VOCAL PROCESS
MUSCULAR PROCESS
VOCAL LIGAMENT
CRICOTHYROID LIGAMENT
CRICOID CARTILAGE
TRACHEA

RIGHT LATERAL ASPECT

SAGITTAL SECTION

©CIBA

Plate IV. Cartilages of the larynx.

second passing from the vocal cords (technically these are folds). The normal human voice potentially embraces a range of at least three octaves of these pitches.

The vocal folds extend horizontally from the front to the rear of the larynx. Anteriorly they are attached to the inner side of the thyroid cartilage which is readily recognized as the "Adams's Apple" in the male (shown in Color Plate I). Posteriorly, each cord is associated with its arytenoid cartilage, the paired cartilages being mounted on the back part of the cricoid cartilage (Color Plate I). It is known that for sound to be produced, the cords must be brought closely together before air is passed between them. As described in the chapter on Support, they are brought together by the action of the arytenoid cartilages which, in reflex to opposition of the breathing muscles, each rotate about a vertical axis to effect the closure (Color Plate I). Thus, when the cords are open, as they are during breathing, they form the shape of a "V" (Color Plate IIa). When the glottis is closed, the cords are positioned for phonation (Color Plate IIb).

Within each vocal cord are two sets of tensor muscles which cooperate to produce the proper amount of tension, and possible length, of the participating cord for each pitch desired. All other factors remaining equal, doubling the length of a string will drop the pitch one octave, and decreasing the weight of the string by one half will raise the pitch one octave. However, the pitch will vary as the square of the tension applied to it. The reader is not to think that the vocal cords act like the strings of a banjo or harp, but the sequence of air waves passing through them is related to the physical principles illustrated by a vibrating string.

Vocal cords (or folds) are capable of changing rapidly in thickness, length, and tightness. The manner in which the edges move to emit the tiny puffs of air cannot, of course, be visualized by the naked eye. However, high-speed motion pictures have shown this action very clearly (Fig. 1, page 12). A change in the effective length of the cords is emphasized by Jackson. Dr. Jackson holds that the edges of the vocal cords become harder with increasing rates of vibration. The ventricular bands (Fig. 9, page 32) have also been assigned a possible cooperative role by Jackson. In fact, individuals who have lost the function of their vocal cords are still able to make sounds by passing air over these membranes. A very clear description of the anatomical features of the larynx is given by Lithgow.[9]

However, for true pitch to be achieved by the singer, still other parts of his vocal assembly must be brought into play. These are the resonating chambers of the pharyngeal and nasal cavities. The pitch produced when one blows into a bottle has little relation to the person who does the blowing. As a resonating chamber, the bottle takes all the wave lengths of the incoming air and selects those that meet the periodicity of its dimensions. Other pitches are muffled out. It follows then that a singer who produces a given pitch in the region of the larynx must utilize his resonating chamber (or chambers, see page 42) in such a manner that he reinforces this particular pitch. If he fails to do this, he will damp out his original tone, and may even produce a sound that is of a pitch other than the one intended. Along with this, it is imperative that the fundamental of a given pitch be always stronger than any of its overtones (the fundamental being the meat in the vocal sandwich).

In the latter part of this chapter, the phenomenon of resonance will be discussed further, with more detailed attention being given to the roles of the pharynx, soft palate, tongue, and mouth.

VOWELS AND CONSONANTS

The fundamental sound of any given pitch is accompanied by a series of overtones. For example, at C one octave below middle C, when the vocal cords are moving at 128 vibrations per second, the first overtone is at middle C (256 vibrations per second). This formula is repeated over and over again until the C two octaves above middle C (1024 vibrations per second) is attained. When such a large family of overtones is set into vibration in the pharynx, not all of them will be damped out, with the result that a type of vowel is always present. That is to say, the sound is not absolutely pure. The singer has only to favor certain of these reverberations (as if he were calling into play certain of the various partials offered on the same fundamental by a Hammond organ) in order to shape a new vowel. At the same time he must not disturb the resonance chamber to the extent that he wavers off the basic pitch, which is the frequency of the fundamental, the lowest of the harmonic series.[10] For purposes of illustration, let the reader imagine a neutral vowel. A neutral vowel is changed to a definitive vowel by movement of the tongue, a major portion of which constitutes the front, and only, adjustable wall of the pharyngeal resonating chamber. This chamber, however, should be changed to only a minor extent for any given vowel since gross movement of the tongue would disturb the resonance chamber to such a degree that the fundamental pitch would fail to be adequately reinforced. It will be noted that on very high notes, definitive vowels are absent or poorly formed. This is due to the fact that the resonance chambers for these pitches are above the level of the tongue.

A look into the mouth during phonation will reveal that the tongue changes very little (about 1/32 to 1/16 of an inch) throughout the singer's entire repertoire of vowels. It will be observed to raise highest for the "e" vowel (Fig. 11b, page 49), to be somewhat lower for "a," and lower still for the "ah" sound. For the shaping of other vowels, the tongue changes very little from the position where the correct "ah" has placed it.

Many singers, and their instructors as well, would give their right arms if songs could be sung without words or vowels. To the aspiring singer vowels spell "trouble." The vowel will not be well-shaped unless the tongue is free from the tensions imposed by the mylohyoid muscle and, indeed, unless the tongue is completely relaxed except for the actual muscles necessary for the position and movement desired. The situation is analagous to that of the leg muscles in a well-trained runner. Running is carried out most efficiently when the various muscles in the leg have "learned" to relax when they are not being employed. Hence, they do not oppose the action of the muscles that are necessary for the movement and have an opportunity to recover before they themselves are called upon to exert a pull. (The reader is referred to page 51 for the important exercises that will assist in the development of free movement of the tongue.)[11]

It is essential that room and flexibility be maintained in the major resonating cavity, the pharynx: The reader may not be aware that under normal conditions most of the tubes of the body (blood vessels, intestines, etc.) are collapsed unless filled. The pharynx falls more or less into this category. Therefore, the singer must train himself to maintain a larger than normal space therein without foreign tension. The position of the mouth and the jaw are major factors in the maintenance of the maximum pharyngeal space which is necessary for the production of correct vowels. But, it should be emphasized that the condition of the jaw (freedom from tension) is more important than its position. In the studio, the author always places his right hand over the beginner's jaw holding the mouth freely open and at the same time, keeping it relaxed (Fig. 15 and 16a, pages 89, 91).

Generally speaking, when one works with a young singer, in which case there has been no vocal abuse, and when the above approach is used in conjunction with vigorous sound, the proper reflexes become automatic through the process of muscle memory. There are exceptions. Some individuals who have sung with "tight" jaws over a period of years must give this matter more serious attention. They should frequently stretch and unhinge the jaw (opening the mouth as far as possible) as an exercise directed toward maximum stretching of the muscles associated with this portion of the face. A little depression can be felt just in front and slightly above the ear lobe when the jaw is completely open but loose.

Consonants are far less troublesome than vowels. They are formed by combined action of the mouth, lips, tongue, teeth, and palate. Whereas, the vowels are vocal, that is, they can only be produced if the vocal cords are vibrating, consonants are produced without the participation of the vocal cords. For example, the "s" sound is a hiss, the "r-rrr" a trill of the tongue. This means that the consonants are actually "noises," and when they are uttered, the vocal flow is momentarily interrupted. They should be produced quickly and yet not so abruptly as to disturb vocal quality. They are valuable in song for reasons of punctuation and completion of words. One of the author's early teachers put it this way: "The vowel is the road you travel on; the consonant is the sign post."

It can now be appreciated that the upper part of the singing apparatus is a trio of components: (1) the vocal cords, which are the regulators of the number of puffs of air per second entering the resonators, (2) the pharynx and nasal cavities which are the major resonators, and (3) the mouth, lips, tongue, teeth, and palate, which participate in the formation of necessary noises, that is, consonants. These components are closely interdependent. For example, if the vibrations of the vocal cords are correctly elicited in accordance with Support, as described in

Chapter 1, and if there is no interference from muscles close to the larynx (primarily the mylohyoid), there is every chance that the vowel instruments (the pharynx, tongue, and soft palate) will be ready to respond to the will of the singer. With these two elements functioning smoothly, the consonants should be readily manageable. In fact, most singers need to be restrained from placing too much vocal quality into certain of their consonants.

THE RESONATORS

As previously mentioned, if a mixture of sound waves is introduced into a chamber or tube, such as the pharynx (Fig. 10, page 43, this structure will tend to reinforce one or more of the waves selectively as a function of its shape.[12] The physical explanation is that many of the vibrations forced upon the system (those possessing the proper period of wave length) will be changed to the natural vibrations of that system, whereas vibrations lacking the proper "period" or common unit of wave length, will be diffused and hence muffled. In addition, if the resonating chamber is shaped like, or fitted to, a megaphone (that is, the mouth), the sound waves emitted will not be spread as from a point, in every direction, but will be focused and thus projected along a defined path. The initial energy of any total of vibrations is not increased as a result of resonance or focusing. It is always decreased by both processes. But amplifications of given sounds, and this over a relatively narrow trajectory, can be achieved. To the listener who is sitting in the "line of fire" it matters little if some original energy is being dissipated; he is experiencing a much louder sound (up to three hundred times louder) than if resonance and projection were not being applied.

Of course, a good resonator system should be as efficient as possible in terms of total energy loss and selective amplification. A unique example of how well such a system can work is provided by the bullfrog. This amphibian fills the Louisiana swamplands with a distinctive bellow that can be heard for hundreds of yards. The vocal feat is accomplished by a pair of adjustable air sacs communicating with the pharynx. Air is passed from lungs to sacs and expelled from sacs to lungs, back and forth over the vocal cords, producing sounds as it passes in both directions, and amplifying these in the elastic sacs which are extremely efficient resonators. The result when multiplied by a few bullfrogs can be quite deafening!

Three different chambers serve to varying degrees as resonators for the human voice. These are shown in Figure 10 and include:

1. The pharynx
2. The nasal cavities
3. The mouth

For practical purposes the pharynx can be subdivided into three resonating chambers: the laryngopharynx, beginning immediately above the vocal cords; the oropharynx, straight behind the mouth; and the nasopharynx. (The laryngopharynx may extend into the region of the oropharynx.) The oropharynx is primarily employed for resonance of tones in the octave between middle C and the C one octave above. In this octave, resonance is also provided in part by the nasal cavities. The sharing of resonance by these two chambers for tones between middle C and an octave above middle C is especially critical and will be discussed in detail in Chapter 4. At this point

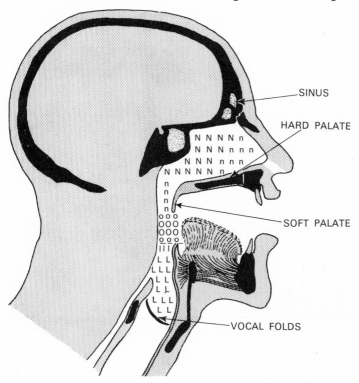

Fig. 10. View of resonating chambers. L = Indicates laryngopharynx. Reinforcements are for low tones. O = Oropharynx. Resonator for tones up to middle C. 264 vibrations per second. N = Nasopharynx and nasal cavities. Resonator for tones from middle C-sharp and up. With the soft palate open, "O" and "N" can combine to obtain the desired frequencies.

it will only be stated that incrementive sharing of resonance by the above-mentioned two resonance chambers
over this octave is necessary to provide a smooth transition in quality from the tones below middle C into this
octave and also upward from this octave. Tones below
middle C require increasingly more resonance throughout
the oropharyngeal region until finally, the laryngopharynx
is involved. In heavy bass notes the laryngopharynx provides most of the resonance reinforcement of the tone.

Because a considerable portion of the pharyngeal
wall (forward) is provided by the back of the tongue
(Fig. 11b, page 49), and because the tongue can be
moved in a controlled manner, the pharynx is an adjustable resonator. This property of the pharynx permits both
gross and fine resonance adjustments to be made, and the
making of these will be discussed further on in this
chapter.

Tones above one octave above middle C require
more and more nasopharyngeal or nasal resonance. Because of its relatively small size and the presence in it
of many jagged corners, bizarre caverns, and outcrop-
pings, air waves of high frequency can be reinforced in
this chamber. Although it is primarily a fixed resonator,
entry to it is dependent on a lowered soft palate. Failure
to drop the soft palate results in the blockage of the resonator with the result that high notes will be weak or
strained. Development of the ability to consciously lower
the soft palate is facilitated by certain exercises. One of
these is to assume a humming position as shown in Fig.
19a (page 101), jaws opened as far as possible with the

lips closed. In another exercise the pupil sings with mouth wide open but with the teacher's hand tightly over it (Fig. 18a, page 100) for the first two notes of a triad; the hand is suddenly released on the third note (Fig. 18b), and if the palate is open, a firm ringing sound will emerge. (Breathing through the nose as well as the mouth is helpful in maintaining the opening between the soft palate and the back of the throat.) The pupil continues to sing and has the experience of feeling resonance in the nasal cavities. It is impossible to keep the soft palate closed while humming in this manner. The superb soprano Emma Calvé is said to have practised two hours each day with the mouth closed.

When a singer's voice sounds weak, even at a distance of a few feet, it may be that he is attempting to use his mouth as a major resonator. The mouth is not a good resonator because its walls are too flexible and too changeable for consistent reinforcement, and it is neither located nor shaped properly. Individuals who employ the mouth as their main resonator are invariably poor singers having short ranges as well as poor quality. They complain that their high notes are not free, and that they become hoarse. In most cases, they are limited to a range of little over an octave and a half, and demonstrate at least three different qualities of sound within this range.

One reason that the singer may be forced to use his mouth as a resonator is that he cannot use his pharynx because of distortion of that chamber by interfering muscles—those which should be used only for the act of swallowing. (This phenomenon will be considered in more detail later.) Another reason is that the singer may be attempting to form the vowels (required for word production) with his mouth. Although this would appear on the surface to be a perfectly reasonable thing to do, it is not the proper way. Vowels should be formed closer to the point of origin. The correct cavity for the formation of a vowel, if the sound is to be heard at a distance, is the pharynx. This leaves the mouth free to remain open and to act in conjunction with the pharynx as a megaphone. If a singer's voice sounds strong at a distance of five feet but is weak at fifty feet, his mouth is not fulfilling its role as a megaphone, even though his basic voice may not be lacking in resonance.

A very important point in any consideration of resonance is that the aspiring student of voice is usually unaware of the necessity of achieving as open a throat as possible during phonation, with a minimum of interference on the part of antagonistic muscles. Not only vocal scientists but also those teachers who have achieved success by means of trial and error agree completely on this point. In the course of various daily activities the throat must assume different shapes. During speech, for example, it is not open as required for singing. Until the singer has acquired the ability to maintain a very large cavity from the level of the vocal cords and upward (without interference from muscles of the neck, jaw, and tongue), little progress in the development of adequate resonance will be forthcoming.

To summarize: Every pitch in a singer's range, except the very highest ones, should have a resonator which matches it perfectly and which can change to form the various vowels (partials) required within that pitch. The pharynx is the only instrument capable of meeting these demands. (Note that little or no vowel formation is possible on pitches from high C and above where the fixed nasal resonator assumes the larger role.) When the pharynx is properly opened,[13] a space extends some three to four inches upward from the vocal cords. Utilization of spaces closer to the vocal cords means that the sound waves will be reinforced more efficiently than if they were required to travel into the oral cavity before being resonated, and also that the mouth can be adjusted into the shape of a megaphone rather than a resonator. The sum of both of these advantages is evidenced by greater volume and more carrying power.

THE ROLE OF THE TONGUE IN ADJUSTING THE RESONATOR

In order for the pharyngeal cavity to be geometrically oriented for resonance, the tongue must extend straight upward from the hyoid bone about 1½ inches.[14] (Fig. 11b, page 49). This position of the tongue can be observed by the singer if he looks into a mirror while forming the vowel "ā" (not "ah") or "ee" with an open mouth. It can be appreciated that the back and side walls of the pharyngeal cavity are relatively fixed. It is mainly the front wall, when it is formed by the tongue's being in proper position, which is the moveable part.

Vowels are partials of the fundamental pitch which

are formed by adjustments of the resonating chambers. The manner by which a singer should shift from one vowel to another is to change the contour of the tongue slightly, usually only ⅓₂ or ¹⁄₁₆ of an inch. In correct phonation 90 to 95 per cent of the vowel sound is formed in the region of the pharynx. The remaining 5 to 10 per cent is formed by slight alterations of the oral or mouth cavity. (Consonants are formed in the mouth, chiefly by the tongue and lip position, but in any event, consonants are noises!) Consequently, when the singer finds that one vowel carries well and another vowel on the same pitch fails in its carrying power, he knows that his immediate source of trouble is the tongue.[15] This instrument is not in correct position. Underlying this fault is either (1) a conscious or unconscious effort to form the major part of the vowel in the mouth or (2) incomplete relaxation of muscles prone to interfere with tongue action.

The tongue and only the tongue can shape the main resonator (the pharynx). It can be called the steering apparatus of the voice. In fact, it regulates two things simultaneously: the reinforcement of a vibrating column of air and the partial quality of the vibration (vowel formation).

The tongue also can—and should—be positioned in such a way that the pharyngeal region and the mouth cavity together form an effective megaphone. A megaphone is small at the mouth and then extends out in the form of a cone containing angles of from 25 to 35 degrees. In order for the pharynx and mouth to form a cavity of this general shape, the tongue must rise straight up releasing the mylohyoid muscle and positioning the hyoid bone

½ inch above the level of the chin (Fig. 11b). As shown in the picture labeled "wrong" (Fig. 11a), the tongue leans back into the throat closing the pharynx and the mylohyoid muscle is pulling the hyoid bone below chin level. This is a common fault, especially if the subject cannot sing high notes. Many singers use the mouth incorrectly as a megaphone. For example, a singer who sings a *fortissimo* on an upper pitch with too much interference

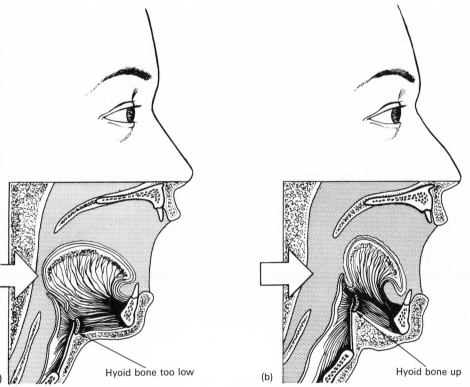

Hyoid bone too low   (b)   Hyoid bone up

Fig. 11. Tongue Positions. **a.** WRONG. Grooved tongue, closing pharynx, mylohyoid pulling hyoid bone below chin level. **b.** CORRECT. Tongue up, pharynx open.

(tension on the larynx) cannot diminish his sound correctly when he desires to do so. He, therefore, closes his lips to make the mouth of the megaphone smaller. By this process he does not diminish the tone, but smothers it.

Actually, the tongue, with its many muscles can adapt itself into more specific shapes and positions than

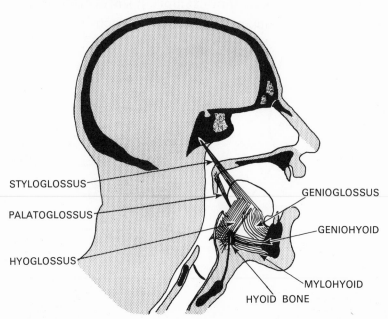

Fig. 12. Major muscles involved in control of tongue, hyoid bone, and soft palate.

are readily conceivable. Its telescopic properties are remarkable. When pushed out over the teeth it can become very long, and by contracting certain groups of muscles it becomes very short. Inervations of the tongue muscles are all supplied by branches of the hypo-glossal or twelfth cranial nerve. During song, tongue movements are mainly effected by five muscles including: the genioglossus, genio-hyoid, hyoglossus, styloglossus, and palatoglossus (Fig. 12).

Another muscle, which is in reality not a tongue muscle, but extends from the chin to the hyoid bone, exerts an adverse effect upon phonation when contracted. This is the mylohyoid muscle, one of the main interfering muscles referred to in the chapter on Support (Fig. 2a, page 14). It can be felt by the reader if he will place his thumb under the chin and yawn deeply. Tension created in this muscle will push the thumb downward. Unless the mylohyoid is relaxed during singing, the tongue muscles cannot carry out their required functions of resonance or vowel formation. Further, tension on this muscle will interfere with the sustained closure of the glottis. It presses the hyoid bone down and opposes the action of the arytenoid cartilages.

THE TONGUE EXERCISE

Because the tongue is such a complicated structure, it has often been termed the "unruly" member of the human body. Unruly or not, it can be tamed just as the fingers can be trained to play the piano. The secret is to develop the ability to move the tongue (rapidly or slowly) at will, back and forth in the mouth while keeping the jaw perfectly relaxed and motionless. All this takes is practice and lots of it. If any of the great singers were called upon to demonstrate this exercise, they would be able to do so immediately, even if they had not consciously attempted it before.

If the singer with poor vocal production finds that while singing he cannot move his tongue back and forth and control his soft palate at will with a motionless jaw he has the clue to a great part of his trouble. He should spend some time every day attempting to develop these abilities. It may be several months before he can achieve motion of the tongue with the jaw perfectly relaxed. However, once he can move his tongue at any desired speed while singing, at the same time retaining a motionless jaw, he will begin to develop with rapidity. One of the remarkable effects arising from a combination of the successfully executed tongue exercise (moving it back and forth rapidly) and phonation is the singer's sensation of a very live ringing quality to the voice. Also, the soft palate becomes more manageable with a free tongue. In fact, it tends to stay down. When the singer is first beginning to experience the above-mentioned "ring," it may disappear when he ceases to move his tongue. When this occurs it is likely that the soft palate has slipped upward, closing off the passage to the nasal resonators. As the exercise is repeated over and over again in practice, the ringing sensation (perfect resonance) will eventually be present even when the tongue is immobile.

For this exercise,[16] the tongue must be comfortably relaxed but high in the mouth. If one observes singers who show outstanding voice production, he will perceive that the tongue is always as it is when one is producing the vowel "ā" with the mouth wide open (Fig. 11b, page 49).

chapter three
THE LARYNX

STRUCTURE OF THE LARYNX

Much has already been said about the various structures that are housed within the larynx. The positioning and activation of the vocal cords (or folds) by the arytenoid cartilages has been treated in detail in Chapter 1 (see Fig. 1, page 12, and Color Plate I). It must now be emphasized that the functions of vocal cords and arytenoid cartilages are greatly dependent on the framework of cartilage and muscle which serves as their support. It is natural that this support be flexible but not too loose. When the vocal cords are contracting, the support must be rigid enough to afford some opposition. The cricothyroid muscle (see Color Plate III) permits the application of various degrees of tension on the cords independently of the muscles within the cords, but the cricoid and thyroid cartilages must themselves be of a definite elasticity for best results.

At birth, the larynx consists of very soft cartilage and connective tissue. It is as pliable as putty. By the time an individual has reached the age of ninety, practically all of this cartilage has ossified so that it is usually grossly inflexible. It might be thought that since ossification is inevitable, some deterioration of the voice after middle age is also inevitable. Actually, the laryngeal cartilages of an individual who has consistently sung, and sung correctly, are usually relatively flexible as compared to those of non-singers in the same age bracket. Nature cooperates to a large degree to fulfill the purpose of any exercise, but regression is rapid when exercise is neglected. For example, if a person is bedridden for any length of time, the bones demineralize (osteoporosis) and the muscles lose their tone, grow weak, and waste away (atrophy) with the result that the legs are no longer as strong as they were during exercise.

The important role which the support of the laryngeal box plays in voice production has been illustrated in spectacular fashion by one of the author's students. This woman exhibited a thyroid deficiency and possessed very soft cricoid and thyroid cartilages. It is possible that the two conditions were related. When she sang A-flat to G (below middle C) her voice held; but below G the thyroid cartilage actually invaginated so that a depression could be felt where the point of the Adam's apple usually protrudes. In addition, the wings of the thyroid cartilage were spread out on either side rendering the voice box quite flat. The voice disappeared altogether under these conditions.

On one occasion the author carried out an experiment in which he had this woman sing while he manually kept the wings of the thyroid from spreading laterally. Under these circumstances she was able to extend her range downward to low E with no difficulty. During subsequent weeks of training, some additional rigidity of the larynx superstructure was developed with the result that her range was extended downward.

POSITION OF THE LARYNX

The correct position of the larynx has long been a subject of debate. The singer has been told that for certain notes it should be up, and for other notes it should be down. In some cases, he may have noted obvious contradictions and differences of opinions among his teachers.

On the basis of extensive critical observation, the author can only conclude that, when Support is correctly applied and interference is absent, the larynx acts as if it had a mind of its own. Under these ideal conditions this organ orients itself automatically so as to render the voice clear and free. Nearly always, it is observed to be in a lowered position during the utterance of a correct sound. During a recent conference with Mr. W. Ruth in Berlin, dozens of X-ray pictures were reviewed that had been taken of many famous singers singing over wide ranges.

Those with the most uniform voice throughout the entire range demonstrated the following larynx positions:

1) The larynx was down on all tones high and low.
2) The top of the larynx did not lean forward or backward for high tones.
3) The larynx and hyoid bone did not press together at any time.

The existence of a space between the hyoid bone and larynx appears to be the most important factor (Fig. 2b, page 14).

Muckey has stated, "The correct action of the voice mechanism consists in the unhampered vibration of the vocal cords, the free motion of the cartilages and muscles of the larynx and full use of the resonant space. This action gives the natural voice or the voice which nature intended, a particular mechanism to produce. Any muscular contraction which prevents the unhampered vibration of the vocal cords, the free motion of the cartilages and the muscles of the larynx or full use of the resonance space is termed an interference." [17]

Although this information appears to have been unnoticed for over half a century, it almost certainly provides the clue to the natural positioning of the larynx during phonation. Under circumstances of complete relaxation, the thyroid cartilage is observed to be between one-half and three-quarter inches below the hyoid bone (Fig. 2b, page 14). During the act of swallowing, the distance is lessened (Fig. 2c). While the singer is inhaling, his larynx drops as low as is physically possible. If his vocal condition is normal, he will note that while making a moaning sound or engaging in a hearty laugh, the larynx will lower itself about one-half inch. The larynx will also be observed to be in this state of adjustment if the singer is performing with correct Support, and his tones are large and clear. These observations point to the conclusion that when the larynx is down and away from the hyoid bone, the vocal cords are free of extraneous strains and are in a position to adjust to the precise tensions required. Conversely, when the larynx is pressing against the hyoid bone (Fig. 2a and c) these conditions do not obtain, and definite evidence of interference is being manifested.[18]

Sometimes a singer who is experiencing vocal difficulty exhibits no space between his thyroid cartilage and the hyoid bone during most phases of vocal production. Although such a severe condition is unusual, the reader may wish to make a test that will establish his own condition in this regard: He should take a breath and place his finger at the point of the Adam's apple. If, when vocalizing, the larynx is observed to rise and close the distance between this cartilage and the hyoid bone above, he can be reasonably certain that his phonation is incorrect. Another clue to the presence of interfering muscle activity is the perception of uncomfortable tensions in the throat during the act of singing.

These phenomena are no doubt due to encumbering actions of the swallowing muscles (including the mylohyoid, muscles of the tongue, the jaw, or the face). To determine whether or not the former are the sources of interference in his own case, the reader may open his mouth and place the index finger and the thumb on the cheeks on either side. If, when he pushes the insides of his cheeks between the upper and lower teeth and begins to make a sound, the attack engenders a feeling of biting the cheeks, he will know that the swallowing muscles are incorrectly involved in the act of phonation.

To experience the correct feeling, the following two steps should be carried out in succession. First, the student should apply Support as described in Chapter 1. Second, he should insert his cheeks between his teeth as in the experiment above. If he now emits a sound of a reasonably easy pitch in the middle of the voice range, all the while striving to keep his jaw motionless in order not to bite his cheeks, this tone should not be felt at the level of the throat. The first sounds may not even approach the quality of those notes produced by the singer while performing incorrectly. But once he has experienced a sound that is not felt in the throat, he is on his way to something better. It could be that the reader has always sung in this manner, or that he is one of the fortunate few who possess a fine natural coordination. If this is the case, he is to be congratulated but also forewarned against the insidious intrusion of bad habits. He should ever be on guard to ensure that muscles prone to interfere be completely relaxed.

On occasion, cases of laryngeal spasm were observed in this studio so severe (the thyroid cartilage being held rigidly against the hyoid bone) that the author felt compelled to massage away or forcibly free the Adam's apple from its position hard against the hyoid bone.[19] It has been his experience that singers who have subjected their throats to unusual abuse over long periods of time may respond positively after weeks or months of daily manipulating; and that, indeed, the correctly indoctrinated singer will benefit from an occasional manual positioning. The principle involved in this type of treatment is analogous to that of massaging the muscles of an athlete. Of course, for both singer and athlete, there can be very little beneficial result if the subject insists on remaining tense.

In this chapter the swallowing muscles as a group have been indicted for being largely responsible for raising the larynx against the hyoid bone. Certain of the tongue muscles are implicated in this act, but not all of them. The jaw and facial muscles are also active during swallowing. To prove this to himself the reader need only place a finger between his teeth and swallow. He will note that he bites his finger and puckers his lips hard around it at the same time that his larynx rises up against the hyoid bone. A stiff jaw, as in swallowing, will nearly always lift the larynx and close the glottis simultaneously.

This is the stuff that interference is made of. It explains why sounds can be made with improper support— but never correct sounds without correct Support.

chapter four

THE REGISTER

"THE BOTTLENECK OCTAVE"

After bitter experience, most teachers and singers have concluded that the basic voice consists of more than one register. As already seen in Chapter 3, this happens because the muscles within the larynx are not properly coordinated over a critical range, and sharing of resonators is neglected over this same range.

The true potential of the human voice can best be demonstrated (and understood) with the young, healthy, large voice that has had no training whatsoever. In this case, the female singer will usually show a brilliant high tone around the upper G, top of the staff, and a dark, coarse, almost masculine sound two octaves below that

G. At this stage it is possible to observe easily the quality
of two different voices. These two different tone qualities
at the opposite ends of the untrained, but potentially coordinated, voice form the basis for much misunderstand-
ing and confusion. The tones described at the opposite
ends of the voice are, of course, produced by predominant
use of different groups of muscles within the larynx and
vocal cords, and by different resonance adjustments. In
the past the lower tones have been called the "chest register" or the "lower register," the upper tones have been
called the "upper register" or the "falsetto" or "head
voice." In the following paragraphs they will be referred
to merely as "the lower" and "the upper."

The powerful, coarse, lower tones in the female
lower voice and the bright, ringing, upper tones two octaves higher indicate a good potential. When the muscles
within the larynx that produce these sounds are properly
coordinated within themselves and there is correct resonance, a sound of great beauty is produced. When improperly used and abused, they create multiple tone
qualities, hoarseness, breathiness, shallowness, shrillness,
and general weakness of voice. For example, the singer
who constantly employs improper resonance may, by pulling the larynx out of normal position, produce a gamut
of nearly two octaves of sounds. However, this mode of
tone production always demonstrates a variety of faults:
(1) In the middle of the short range there will usually be
four or five pitches that are very weak. (2) The overall
voice is lacking in natural quality, particularly the four
or five pitches mentioned. (3) The true vibrato is of

necessity destroyed. (4) There is trouble with hoarseness and laryngitis. (5) When the singer should be at the peak of his career, his voice is gone.

The two distinctly different qualities in the young, powerful, untrained voice indicate that before the overall quality can be more uniform, there must be some kind of cooperation between the two. How to effect a smooth transition from one end of a singer's range to the other is the main subject of this chapter and perhaps the most important single concept in the book.

Assuming that all the component parts of the vocal instrument are properly aligned, the following will be found to obtain:

1) The Support muscles have complete control of the larynx, and all the adjustments therein for specific speeds of vibration may be applied consistently and without interference.

2) Employment of the Support muscles facilitates control over the adjustments of the resonators.

Under these conditions a sharing of muscles within the vocal cords and of resonators can be made to produce tones intermediate to "upper" and "lower."

Tones one octave above middle C and upwards require more and more nasopharynx resonance or the tone becomes more and more falsetto in quality (Fig. 10, page 43). Therefore, if any singer, male or female, sings with the soft palate closed between the two C's, from middle C upward one octave, there are two alternatives—both wrong: (1) The singer can resort to the use of forced resonance with resulting strain and abuse to the larynx.

(2) He can shift to more and more falsetto quality, as demonstrated by poorly trained female singers. Indeed, it is now apparent that the factor which creates *the main difference between male and female quality is the opening and closing of the soft palate.* This is a very important finding! Most female singers close the soft palate from the A 440 upward even when they open it properly from middle C 264 up to A 440.

Because the frequency becomes more rapid the higher one sings, the short waves pass through the laryngopharynx and oropharynx without being amplified until they reach the nasopharynx where a resonator can be found to match the faster frequency. In the middle of the octave between the two C's, which is approximately F-sharp, the resonators should share the reinforcement of sound at about a fifty-fifty rate, that is coupling the laryngopharynx with the oropharynx plus the nasopharynx in this ratio. Many singers, who are unaware of this principle, tighten laryngeal and pharyngeal muscles in an effort to squeeze the large resonators down to meet the fast frequency of high tones. When the proper resonator for the short waves, or the fast frequency, is opened correctly (by lowering the soft palate and pulling it away from the back wall of the throat), the singer does not need to strain because he has a resonating cavity ready to adjust for the desired pitch. If a conscious effort is made to select the proper resonator, the necessary muscular adjustments within the larynx appear to take place automatically. It is an empirical fact, however, that without correct laryngeal muscular leverage and without proper pharyngeal, epipharyngeal, and oral resonance adjustment, the desired results will not be forthcoming. On the basis of the foregoing, it is more easily understood why the improperly trained singer encounters so much difficulty between the two C's. For instance, even if the adjustment within the larynx were completely correct, if the resonator needed to amplify and beautify the sound is closed, it becomes physically impossible to arrive at the desired result. As indicated previously, a practical maneuver is to advise the young singer that arriving at the proper tone quality between the two C's is more a matter of resonating adjustment than it is of vocal strength. However, before adjustments can be made in either vocal cord musculature or choice of resonating chamber, correct Support must be achieved.

What has been said about the muscles within the larynx has long been established and accepted. Understanding of the pedagogical techniques that must be employed to bring about an effective and smooth coordination on the part of these muscles, as demonstrated by the vocal techniques of the great singers, has been the author's main goal, and he would not be writing a book at this time unless he felt that this mission has been accomplished.

The chart in Fig. 13 illustrates to what extent the respective muscles within the larynx (those which govern all "upper" and all "lower") and the respective resonating chambers are utilized for given tones. Note that *cooperation* is necessary to produce proper phonation in both male and female voices. It should be noted also that in

CORRECT LARYNGEAL AND RESONANCE SHARING FOR ALL VOICES

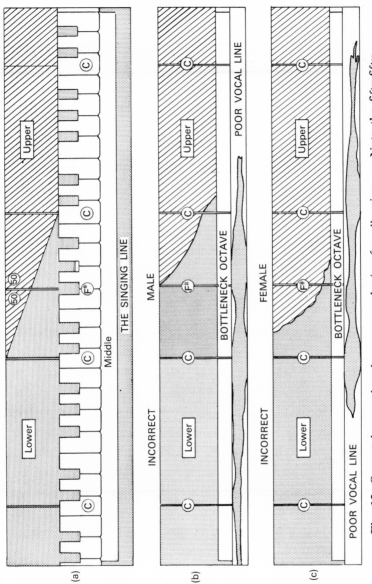

Fig. 13. Correct laryngeal and resonance sharing for all voices. **a.** Note the fifty-fifty sharing of both the resonance and vocal cord muscles for "upper" and "lower" between the two C's (middle C-264 up one octave). This sharing results in a straight vocal line. **b.** WRONG. Male voice pulling "lower" up to F-sharp. Note distorted vocal line. **c.** WRONG. Female voice attempting to sing with "upper" down to D just above middle C-264. Note weak, distorted vocal line.

the past too much emphasis has been placed upon the muscles within the vocal cords and not enough on the crico-thyroid muscles (which hold the cricoid and thyroid cartilages in proper relative position) and the resonating adjustments. In other words, the larynx adjustment can basically supply only one need, which is to put a column of air into vibration at a given frequency, consisting of a fundamental tone and a series of overtones. When the larynx is asked to do more, interference occurs. The larynx and vocal cord muscles have ample strength in most cases to supply a very wide range of frequencies when not imposed upon to do what the resonators should do, namely, to amplify, to beautify, and to furnish the vowel partials.

The above findings with regard to the tensor muscles within the larynx were established years ago. More recently, it has been found that all voices, male or female, bass or soprano, encounter the greatest difficulties *on exactly the same pitches,* i.e., over the octave from middle C to the C above. This recent discovery has proved to be the key to the problem of establishing a straight vocal line.[20] It clearly establishes the fact that the musculature of the vocal cords and the shapes of the resonance chambers are basically the same in all voices, male and female. It also confirms the ideas developed above with respect to the sharing of the two sets of vocal equipment over the critical octave, and indicates that the sharing must be carried out in the same manner in all voices.

When it is once established in the singer's mind that the pitches from middle C to the C one octave above constitute "a bottleneck" and why (Fig. 13b and c, page 65) considerable progress will be forthcoming. This octave is referred to as "the bottleneck" because over this octave it is possible to make sounds in *many different incorrect ways.* It is the area which is loaded with trouble, *unless coordination by nature, by accident, or by correct vocal training has previously been established.* To say to a singer that both "upper" and "lower" must be used in this octave is of little value because both good and bad singers are doing this already. The important point is *how* the proper adjustment is achieved between these two C's. A major part of the trouble in this critical range is created by the reflex action of the swallowing muscles, which most individuals use to some extent while speaking.[21] Interference occurs the instant the swallowing muscles are engaged because they pull the larynx up against the hyoid bone. The degree to which this takes place determines the extent of the interference. However, there are as many different incorrect combinations possible in this octave as there are incorrectly trained voices. The author has found that *an indispensable factor in the making of sharing adjustments over the "bottleneck octave" is the ability of the singer to keep the soft palate lowered at all times.* Keeping the nasal resonators fully available facilitates all other adjustments.

Most male singers force the resonators for the lower tones far too high (Fig. 13b, page 65). Most female singers attempt to sing down as far as middle C with the resonators of the upper tones (Fig. 13c). As soon as they find the tones too weak, they attempt to get some help from the "lower," but at this point it is too late. This is because the interference created will not allow correct coordination. Therefore, the laryngeal muscles make whatever combination is possible under the prevailing bad circumstances. What is usually not recognized is the fact that the tones are weaker, not because of lack of strength on the part of the larynx but because of lack of reinforcement (resonance). Cooperation of "upper" and "lower" in terms of both resonance and muscle pull, must be established on the basis indicated on the chart, Fig. 13a. *Note the equal sharing at approximately F-sharp.* The percentage of pull and resonance adjustment changes on each succeeding pitch upward or downward is indicated on the chart. Therefore, the tone quality must also change, but only slightly, on each different pitch. While the chart in Fig. 13 is merely a schematic visual aid, it has proven itself to be a definite aid in the developing of many fine voices in the past few years. Since it was originally discovered some years ago that "the bottleneck" is between these two C's in all voices from soprano to bass, many hundreds of voices, from newsboys to outstanding singers, have been tested by the author. Each test has established this principle more firmly. Although the physiological reasons have seemed somewhat obscure, the empirical evidence can no longer be questioned.[22]

One of the important aspects of this finding is that if a great change in quality and power is observed between the lowest and highest notes in an individual's voice, this is due to error and misuse. *Incorrect resonance adjustment makes it impossible for the muscles in the larynx to cooperate properly*. If the muscles that interfere with the smooth and consistent closure of the glottis and correct adjustment of the larynx are applied (as described in Chapter 1), the larynx becomes so badly distorted that the laryngeal and vocal cord muscles, which possess the potential to coordinate the voice, *actively create a large gap in the middle of a natural voice*. Muscles can only produce pulls, and that the powers of the pulls are functions of leverage. A man can move great weights with proper leverage and, conversely, can injure himself while lifting very little if he uses improper leverage. If glottis closure (the bringing together of the vocal folds) is accomplished by any means other than Support (which permits the arytenoid cartilages to hold the cords together at their posterior bases), abnormal positioning of the cords ensues, and the required leverages cannot be forthcoming.[23]

Indeed, experience has shown that when a singer vocalizes with correct Support and the above-mentioned coordinating features are in a proper state of execution (including the lowering of the soft palate so that the nasal resonators are fully available), no need will arise for shifting to so-called falsetto tones between the two C's for any voice, male or female. Only the following will be necessary: a greater intensity for loudness, subdued intensity for softer sounds. All correct tones are produced in the same manner throughout the entire gamut of the voice with the intrinsic vocal muscular network solving the problems easily in all phases of voice production. Under these conditions, the sounds of the upper tones of the male voice, previously called falsetto, *will resemble those of a dramatic soprano from the upper C upward.*[24] Conversely, but in accordance with the same principles, the lower half of the female voice, produced with correct Support and resonance, will have a full, round, and warm sound, like that of the great Ebe Stignani, and a still heavier sound in a heavy contralto voice.

In concluding this chapter the author wishes to leave one main thought in the reader's mind: *To conquer* "the bottleneck octave," *the soft palate must be open all of the time for all voices.*

chapter five
THE VOCAL PARAMETERS

VOLUME, QUALITY AND CONTROL

The purpose of this chapter is to emphasize the close relationship that exists among the vocal parameters: volume, quality, and control. At this point, it is not necessary that "volume" be enlarged upon; and "quality" is also readily understandable. However, "control" does not have substance by itself as do the other two. In fact, one is most likely to notice its absence, particularly with respect to volume or to quality. Still, all of these elements of voice should be developed simultaneously.

Although the young singer with a beautiful but undeveloped voice presents a challenging potential, such a singer is by no means ready for difficult professional work or for heavy choral singing. Despite his opinions and those of his entourage, he is actually undeveloped in terms of volume, quality, and control. As in the case of his athlete counterpart, he has many years of muscle strengthening, as well as muscle coordinating, ahead, if he is to meet the demands of a rigorous career.

One of the ways in which an athlete comes to display superiority (in terms of control, endurance, or efficiency) is to develop the muscles required for his sport above and beyond what normally might be required. Consider the case of the baseball pitcher. In order to obtain control, he must concentrate on two things: (1) developing great power, so much power that there is always some in reserve, (2) establishing the most efficient and consistent throwing patterns for the various types of pitches. There will be a much better chance of his throwing strikes (especially late in the game) if he does not have to be concerned with muscle fatigue or pitching in an unfamiliar manner. A tired set of muscles used in an inconsistent manner cannot be fully responsible to the pitcher's will in terms of control or quality of delivery.

The situation in the case of the neophyte singer is closely analogous to that of the neophyte baseball pitcher. In order to develop a voice that will have persistent good quality, will possess exceptional volume when required, and will respond truly in terms of control, the singer must exercise the singing muscles. The nature of this exercise should be twofold: (1) the student should exercise the *proper* singing muscles, those that with the greatest efficiency will produce tones of pleasing quality over a great range; (2) the student must exercise these muscles vigorously by singing loudly.

The main differences between the conditioning of an athlete and that of a singer are (1) since singing is usually the more complex activity, involving the coordination of more muscles that are not under direct mental control, a longer interval must pass before an acceptable result is obtained; and (2) as mentioned previously, the singer must almost invariably *un*learn certain muscle habits that have developed as a result of his existence in a highly artificial civilization.

Perhaps, if phonetics and language—the means by which men communicate thoughts—had not evolved so rapidly at a rate out of pace with the development of human anatomy, the average voice would be much better coordinated than it is today.

In this regard it is interesting to note that those countries in which the vowels are more sustained in speech (such as Italy, Sweden, and Norway) produce many outstanding singers, but fewer singers originate from countries where consonants are employed in inordinate proportion. Russia and Germany also produce excellent vocal artists, particularly in the lower ranges, quite probably because during speech the larynx is kept low and away from the hyoid bone due to the extraordinarily gutteral phonetics of the languages of these countries. It is of great interest that the Russian singers have developed great high tones as well as low, but Germany has not produced many singers with great high tones. The difference is that German teachers have always discouraged the use of the falsetto in the male voice while in Russia, even today, we hear the male falsetto used with great power in many male choral works.[25] On the other hand, it could not be expected that singers would develop in the Orient who are outstanding in the Western style because there the larynx is too often pressed against the hyoid bone in everyday speech. Singers from Latin countries, such as Spain and South America, exhibit unnaturally shrill and bright voices, due partly to singing tradition, but also possibly to a fiery and emotional temperament which in seeking expression allows interfering muscles to constrict the vocal mechanism.

Of special interest is the controversial Hawaiian tenor and his unusually high range for a male voice. An Hawaiian educator explained that this came about as an emergency measure. When missionaries first arrived in Hawaii, they brought with them four-part church music. Women were not allowed to sing in the early church choirs. Consequently, male falsettos were substituted for both alto and soprano parts. Because of this situation, it became conventional for male singers to sing in this manner—a perfect illustration of how tradition governs behavior.

Since most Americans are positioned somewhere between the above-mentioned extremes of phonetic heritage, the assumption can be made that some incorrect habits have been formed which must be unlearned by the singer before he can begin practicing loudly over long exercises.

Paradoxically, this unlearning is best accomplished by the singer's making loud sounds. If the reader will refer to Chapter 1, he will note that in order to obtain the "feel" of making a proper sound, an abnormally energetic attack is required (such as in barking). This initial phase of singing with proper Support is, however, not carried out over extended periods of time, and actually should be accomplished under the strict guidance of a qualified voice teacher. As evidence that muscles are now being exercised that have not been employed in earlier singing, the student may experience slight soreness and considerable fatigue at first, a condition that disappears rather rapidly. After many months of singing in this manner, the student will note that the upper back has become slightly broader but the overall symmetry of the back will more closely resemble classic proportions in both male and female.

The role of general physical condition in the development of a singer is pertinent to this discussion. It can be appreciated that overall conditioning results in the establishment of muscle tone and stamina, the possession of which cannot help but be of great assistance during voice training, and in a developed singer may mean the difference between an acceptable, correct voice and a great one. Any continuing activity which will, on occasion, tax one almost to the limit of his endurance, such as hiking, running, or swimming, is recommended.[26]

It is of paramount importance that the singer exercise his voice by employing only those muscles which aid in the production of a proper tone. Support—the measured opposition of the breathing muscles—must be the unencumbered driving force that passes air through the larynx and causes the arytenoid cartilages to revolve about bringing together the vocal cords (closing the glottis). The larynx must be low and away from the hyoid bone, not by conscious positioning, but because the mylohyoid muscle at the base of the tongue is completely relaxed allowing the muscles within the vocal cords to set the proper leverage which allows the larynx to find its proper level. Only those tongue muscles that are necessary for resonance adjustments should be under tension, and the body generally must be in a state of maximum efficiency: a relaxed alertness achieved by thorough training and confidence born of experience. Under these conditions the advanced singer should sing loud and often.

The importance of developing volume is illustrated by the often observed phenomenon that a strong voice of good quality can be ruined by the constant use of a microphone. To the singer a microphone is a crutch; the more he uses it, the less he will be exercising his singing muscles. Not only does he allow his muscular tissue to become flabby so that over a period of time he finds that it is no longer possible for him to be heard in a large room without a microphone, but the gaps in his vocal coordination begin to appear soon after his volume drops. Thus, a vicious cycle is set into motion. As the proper singing muscles become weakened by lack of use and are less able to respond to his will the singer, in desperation, brings into play surrounding muscles which unfortunately are not able to take up the slack because the very act of their being under tension interferes with the basic vocal mechanism. The result is analogous to rubbing an eye which is full of sand with intent of relieving the pain. The only result of this action is more anguish.

Great singers who have been able to perform well in their more advanced years have always been individuals who commanded great vocal power. On the other hand, those performers who are recorded as having lost their voices before middle age exhibited smaller voices, not easily heard in large auditoriums and over orchestras. Indeed, continued control of quality is so intimately associated with development of volume and its control that it is practically impossible to consider one without the other.

The reader must not draw the conclusion that only loud singing is beautiful. Many singers with superior quality cannot be heard in the next room. In fact, many young singers exhibit beautiful voices without volume. The important points are (1) that quality goes when volume is added incorrectly, and (2) that quality goes when volume is not developed. The strength of the proper singing muscles must be built up to five or six times their initial strength. When a young singer's quality is good, his necessary coordinations are also largely good, and with only minor modifications he will be ready to begin the development of his muscles so that he will be able to meet the demands of heavy choral loads or continuous professional singing. The singer with good quality but poor volume needs the constant protection and advice of a thoroughly schooled, experienced mentor to develop volume without loss of quality. Possession of control, quality, and volume forecast an ample vocal range.

Many singers are unaware of the essential differences between a vibrato and a tremolo, believing that they are one and the same and that they merely vary in speeds. The fact is that, although they may both be described as pulsations in the voice, they are at extreme ends of a range of magnitude and periodicity. Bad tremolo is the ruination of a voice. The vibrato, on the other hand, is a most important feature of all correct and beautiful singing. It is evidence of quality, the factor which accompanies carrying power; and when it is correct, it is also the guarantee of a long vocal career.

THE TREMOLO

The tremolo is the direct result of incorrect vocal production. It is caused by incorrect breath Support which, in turn, causes constriction of the throat by the major swallowing muscles, those of the tongue being the chief offenders. Interference is brought about by the tongue and the jaw muscles pulling the larynx against the hyoid bone so that it cannot function freely.[27] Tremolo, in the vocal scheme, is analogous to an automobile motor having one dead spark plug—this throws the motor out of balance and causes the car to shake spasmodically. Tremolo is characterized by the following symptoms: (1) a quivering tongue, (2) a jumpy jaw, (3) a shaky larynx. In a bad tremolo all three of the above organs will dance to the tune of the defect. The resulting tone reminds one of the bleat of a sheep or a goat. These quality characteristics occur because the pulsation in the voice is extremely rapid and the main resonators for voice production are largely occluded.

THE VIBRATO

The vibrato is a regular pulsation that transmits a "ring" to the voice, a characteristic that is evident to the educated listener as a sure sign of a healthy voice.

The physical reason for the phenomenon is that tensing of the breathing muscles involved in Support is maintained by impulses sent to the muscles by the nervous system. Although these impulses are individually of very short duration, they are applied at so rapid a rate that the muscles slip only to the slightest degree between stimulations. The better the condition of the breathing muscles and the more correctly experienced the singer, the evener the pulsation and the shorter the lag time between individual contractions. To state it in another way, a sustained tone can be thought of as a string of very short tones. If a picture could be taken in slow motion of a correct vibrato cycle, it would be possible to observe that the tone stops almost completely for a split second, and then sounds again.

When interference from the abdominal muscles is permitted to occur, the rhythm of the contractions is thrown out of cycle and this unevenness is reflected in the voice as an unpleasant wobble. The wobble itself is not a tremolo. It is the vibrato which is out of cycle. The cause of this deficiency is a muscular interference in the Support system rather than in the larynx.[28]

The reader can now appreciate that the vibrato is a desirable quality that *should* be heard in his voice. Some explicit reasons are as follows:

1) It is the most accurate barometer of correct vocal production. (All of the vocal parameters must be coordinated perfectly, or it will not be heard in its proper form.)

2) It lends quality to the voice. No voice can be really beautiful without a ringing vibrato. The tone may be loud and have carrying properties, but without vibrato it sounds "dead." It is often difficult to determine whether it is above or below the intended pitch.

3) When vibrato is present in a voice, the singer possesses great mobility and dexterity. In music that has rapid runs, the singer with correct vibrato moves from one pitch to another in rhythm with the vibrato. The singer without vibrato has difficulty with fast runs. When the vibrato is evident, the singer's tone is as vibrant on a sustained note as it is in movement through several fast passages. In contrast, the voice with the straight tone sounds "dead" on sustained notes, but will give some evidence of life in moving from one pitch to another. The reason for the latter is that Support is of necessity invoked

to get from one pitch to another, once again emphasizing the fact that free vocal cord function is dependent solely on the alert functioning of the respiratory system.

Once one realizes that the pernicious tremolo and the true vibrato are complete opposites, it can further be understood that between two great extremes there is always a common ground from which they start moving their separate ways; i.e., a tremolo can be so mild in some cases that it borders slightly on a vibrato. An excitable individual will sometimes display a vibrato so rapid that it sounds as though it were a tremolo. The chief problem in a case of a mild tremolo is to be able to recognize the difference between vibrato and tremolo. With the chronic tremolo, it is possible to diagnose the cause—and its presence—before the singer sings a note. To be free of tremolo, the throat must be free in the area between the hyoid bone and the larynx. The larynx should be movable and very flexible when not singing. In a bad tremolo the larynx is often pressed completely out of shape.

Recently, a case of tremolo presented itself in our studio (in a normally very fine tenor) where none of the telltale physical signs were apparent. There was no reason for the tremolo, but there it was! The singer's tone quality was poor and characteristically "bleaty." When correct Support was rigorously applied, the quality was at times greatly improved, but the tremolo was never completely conquered. At times this singer could turn the tremolo on and off at will, and at other times it was completely out of his control. So it went, both student and teacher badly perplexed, until one day the tenor was taken to the hospital after collapsing at work. His pulse rate was 180. A medical examination revealed that the thyroid gland was hyperactive, and was over-stimulating the pulse. In a discussion with the physician, it developed that symptoms of this ailment include trembling hands and *tongue*. Here, of course, was the source of the very strange tremolo which refused to be diagnosed by the well-known symptoms.

While the tremolo is always caused originally by a lack of proper vocal Support, it is actually expressed by other components of the singing track. When a singer makes a tone with incorrect Support, the weakest member will be the immediate cause of the tremolo. In some cases, it is the muscle in the base of the tongue. It is, however, most likely to be incorrect coordination on the part of the network of muscles within the larynx itself. It is practically impossible for the muscles of the arytenoid cartilages to do their proper work when Support is not ample, and completely impossible when Support is incorrect.

THE VIBRATO EXERCISE

Knowledge of the origin of the vibrato has given the voice teacher a most valuable tool. Since the on-and-off action of the respiratory system is the cause of the vibrato, activating the Support system on and off slowly becomes a very practical approach to free vocal emission. Not unlike the tongue exercise, this controlled on-and-off action of the breathing muscles with sound gives the same audible result as the slow unpleasant wobble. However, like the tongue exercise, the singer can stop the slow wobble completely or in time bring it up to vibrato speed, at will.

Great care must be taken that the wobble be controlled by the same muscular action as the bark or the correct staccato. The chest must be high, shoulders completely relaxed, and the sound produced by an in and upward movement on the part of the abdominal muscles. A vocal wobble can be produced, particularly in lower tones, simply by pulling the abdominal muscles downward, but this leads to much trouble and should therefore be avoided.

chapter six

THE PRIVATE
LESSON

THE VOICE INSTRUCTOR

When the instructor is thoroughly fortified with correct information in vocal technique, the private lesson is purely a matter of conveying this knowledge to the pupil. His success or failure depends entirely upon his ability to communicate.

Vocal technique can be taught properly only by application—having the student perform in the presence and under the direct guidance of the teacher. This is so because the chief problem in teaching a performing art is communication. Over fifty years ago Dr. Floyd Muckey wrote that the English vocabulary does not describe sound properly; it has not been improved in the interim. Words alone are simply inadequate to convey information which is intended to enable the subject to make choices that involve dozens of voluntary and involuntary muscles. (No one has ever learned to swim by correspondence.) Since words are inadequate, it becomes necessary to employ devices that will get the work done; hence, the private lesson.

The competent vocal instructor is always a good psychologist. For example, he is aware that it is more important not to do and say the wrong things than it is to do and say the right things. It is very easy to confuse singers. In essence, the singer *must* learn to sing from his *own* voice, and the teacher can teach only on the basis of that voice. At the beginning of work with every new pupil, the teacher should always ask himself these questions: What right have I to tell this person how to sing? Have I diagnosed his problem carefully, or does he actually have a problem? Do I have a reasonable understanding of how his mind works? Even if my information is correct, will it mean to him what it means to me, or am I about to make matters worse than they are already? A physician recently told the author, "When I am called in on a case, my greatest responsibility is to be sure that I do not make matters worse than they are already." The vocal teacher has the same responsibility.

Most vocal teachers have had difficulty describing the breathing apparatus to students who are attempting to develop Support. This process can easily be demonstrated by the use of a single mechanical model (Fig. 14a and b). The model is made from a glass bell jar, the mouth of which is covered by a rubber dental dam. From

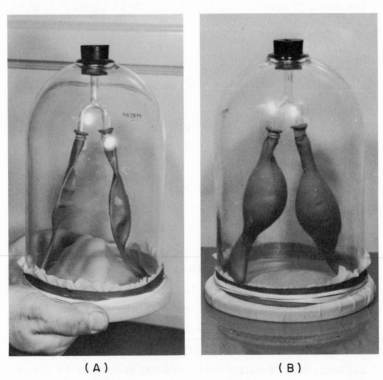

(A)   (B)

Fig. 14. Mechanical model represents breathing apparatus. **a.** When air is expelled, lungs empty, and diaphragm is elevated. **b.** When air fills lungs after deep breath is taken in, diaphragm is lowered.

the top of the jar are suspended two rubber balloons, each attached to an arm of glass Y tube. The balloons represent the lungs, the Y tube represents the trachea and bronchial tubes, the rubber dam represents the diaphragm. When the lungs are relatively empty (the air having been expelled), the diaphragm is elevated in the shape of a dome (Fig. 14a). When the lungs are filled with air following a deep intake of breath, the diaphragm is lowered (Fig. 14b). This position of the diaphragm is also shown in Fig. 3a and is very important in developing Support. Note that this is an example of abdominal breathing. The walls of the glass jar, which represent the rib cage, do not move.

Approximately 20 percent of the students who present themselves for vocal instruction are singing essentially correctly at the time of the initial interview. It is not necessary that these voices follow the complete course outlined in this chapter, although they should be strengthened evenly in all of the vocal parameters (volume, control, and quality) to maintain complete balance. However, if the "bottleneck octave" shows weakness, the procedure given here should be followed. This chapter is intended chiefly as a guide for the instruction of those singers who are not already on the correct vocal track. *It must always be remembered that singing and speaking are not natural functions, but are acquired arts.*

THE AUDITION

The teacher should not make the mistake of starting the first appointment with a long lecture on vocal technique. This only frightens the student. Instead, the pupil should be encouraged to talk at some length, and then be permitted to sing his audition song. Something good must be said about his performance, no matter how poor it might have been. Praise is one of the greatest teaching tools. The most important thing at this point is to rid the pupil of the fear he has of the sound of his own voice. The pupil must be made to be relaxed mentally and bodily. Tenseness can prevent him from understanding what the teacher is saying! The following statement has served the author well: "No matter what you hear, stop worrying. Put the full responsibility on me and let me worry about your voice."

Since control of the student's mental and physical behavior is so important, it makes little sense to have him stand four or five feet away while he is trying to make the sounds the teacher wishes him to make. This problem is easily solved by the following: An adjustable stool is obtained from a medical supply house, one which can be lowered or raised over a range of about a foot. This is placed in front of the piano keyboard with the pupil facing away from the piano. The height is adjusted so that the line from the knees to the body is level (Fig. 4). The teacher's right hand is placed on the pupil's jaw (Fig. 15), with the index finger and thumb extending along the cheeks between the student's teeth (the mouth is wide open). The fourth finger is placed at the point of the larynx between the hyoid bone and the thyroid cartilage. The teacher now has the means to observe the critical muscular movements made by the singer while inhaling and exhaling, and the action of the larynx, jaw, and tongue at the point of phonation. In addition to the above, the pupil should be seated far enough away from the piano so that the spine has to bend back about an inch to touch the piano just below the keyboard (Fig. 4b). He cannot be in the "swayback" position (Fig. 4a) if he is to release the lower abdominal muscles for proper Support.

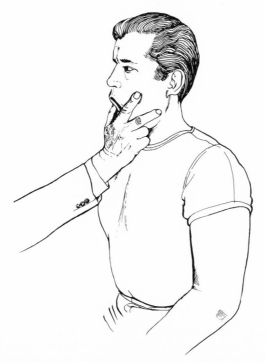

Fig. 15. Singer seated at the piano, back to keyboard, at arm's length from teacher.

THE FIRST LESSON

Since the structure of the larynx and the resonating chambers in the male and female are basically similar, both sexes require similar training. There are, however, two major differences in the anatomy of men and women which cause women to have more difficulty bringing the Support up high enough under the diaphragm. First, they are weaker in muscular development. Secondly, the structure of the female body (for the purpose of childbirth) gives them more room between the pelvic area and the ribs, which makes it more difficult to raise the abdominal bulk high enough under the diaphragm for correct Support. Starting pitches for male and female voices may also be different. This will be explained in greater detail in the section on the male voice.

PEDAGOGY FOR THE FEMALE VOICE

If the reader has not read the preceding chapters carefully, what follows here will place him at a great disadvantage. Prerequisite work, as in all other subjects, is imperative. After the student is properly seated (Fig. 4) and the teacher's hand is placed on the jaw (Figs. 15 and 16a), sound the C one octave above middle C. If and when she is able to contract her abdominal muscles properly (Support), have her do the following: vocalize two staccato notes by sustaining the second attack on the "O" vowel, thus:

If unsuccessful, examine the jaw with the hand (which has remained in position). Move the head gently from side to side until all the neck muscles are completely re-

laxed. The same procedure should again be employed
until at the point of attack the larynx has fallen down and
away from the hyoid bone (Fig. 2b). When this space
remains open during the attack, the sound will be round,

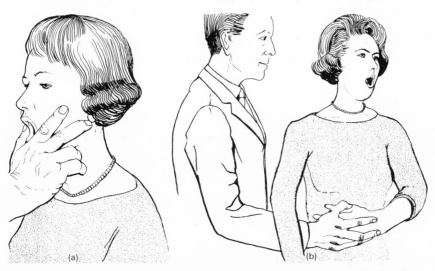

Fig. 16. a. This shows how the teacher can determine with his hand
the relaxation of the jaw, the position of the larynx with his fourth
finger, and tension in the mylohyoid muscle just above the chin.
b. Sitting at the piano, the pupil turns her back to the teacher. He
places his hand over hers (approximately over the navel), and the two
together jerk their hands inward and upward.

full, and dark. If such a sound is produced, proceed
quickly; do four or five of these in a row, then rest for
about ten seconds. Lower the pitch to B-flat. Following
another short rest period, raise the pitch back to C and
finally to C-sharp. Do not move the singer up the scale
to the point where she loses this new free sound she has
just experienced.

Should the effort be persistently unsuccessful, revolve the student a quarter of a turn so that her back is toward the instructor (Fig. 16b) and place the right hand over hers on the lower part of the abdomen. Pull upward together. The pupil will now have to be shown how to hold her own jaw in the correct open position. Employing the same procedure used for Support, sound the same pitch of C, and have the student make another attack on the "O" vowel on the two staccato notes, sustaining the second, with instructor and student jerking with the attacks during phonation. Vibrating the hands and moving them in and upward while the student is sustaining the sound on the second staccato note gives much aid to achieving Support. If this procedure fails, one of two problems exists. Either the pupil is not psychologically or physically prepared to give the desired sound, or she has a very severe case of vocal malalignment. The best way to determine this is to see if the hyoid bone and the larynx separate at the start of inhalation (Fig. 2b). If not, it is possible that they never separate properly. On the other hand, if the larynx is free when the pupil is not singing or speaking, it can be further conditioned by gently moving it up and down. When the larynx does not move freely, the pupil requires special treatment. Reduce the tension in the area between the hyoid bone and the larynx by manipulation without phonation. This procedure has been described in detail by Stanley.[29] When the larynx shows some displacement from the hyoid bone, place the pupil in a horizontal position, and with the assistance of a third party at the piano, follow the procedure outlined in Chap-

ter 1 and shown in Fig. 8. If the case is very severe, as it
often is in a soprano who has sung high notes with a
tremolo, a great deal of work in the horizontal position
is required (1) to acquire the correct Support and (2)
to superinduce the correct nerve and muscular action. No
matter how stubborn the case may be, it must be remembered that it is completely useless to let the student make
sounds with her old tensions and interferences. The author has yet to find a pupil with whom this problem cannot be solved when there is complete cooperation. The
process does, however, involve many hours of painstaking
perseverance.

Now, to return to the more normal case. If the pupil
was able to produce the proper sounds in the upper zone
(C, B, and B-flat, etc.), sound the B-flat below middle C
without revealing to the pupil where the instructor's hands
are on the keyboard. If she is a soprano she has probably
never made a sound on this pitch. Employ the same procedure as before, but bear in mind that the student is now
on her so-called "lower register." If the sound is full, dark,
and powerful (i.e., the opposite of strident, scratchy, and
shrill) and at the same time a space can be discerned between the larynx and the hyoid bone, coordination in the
lower zone has been achieved. Next, skip around in this
area (the same as on the octave above the C, B, and
B-flat) and even to the A and A-flat below, always with
ten seconds of rest between takes. If successful, move
back to "upper" and ascertain if the student can still perform correctly in this area. If the upper tones come in
now as before, the battle is more than half won.

The best procedure the author has found for making progress from this point is to not let the pupil know which notes are being played but move her back and forth on the octave with the same two staccato notes, sustaining the second one. Do this over and over again, *but do not permit her to sing any notes between for some time.* If she has never used her lower tones, or even if she has but produced the sounds in a different way, it would only add confusion to have her sing, for example, a scale on this octave from B-flat to B-flat. This coordination is far too new to respond properly on successive notes up and down a scale.

If successful in the above steps, a worthwhile vocal lesson has been administered. *Instruct the pupil not to try out sounds on her own until the next appointment,* but give an assignment since she must begin to develop Support. Instruct her to develop the muscular strength in the abdominal region by carrying out the rolling motion as described in previous chapters; and have her open her mouth very wide as often as she can during the week while looking into a mirror to see the function of the soft palate and uvula, especially to observe how the space between the uvula and the back wall of the throat can be widened and narrowed at will (Fig. 17a and b). This exercise stretches the muscles so that the mouth can remain open in a relaxed manner. In Figure 17, however, in order to give a better view of the back region of the oral cavity, the tongue is shown lower than is actually recommended for proper phonation. The correct position of the tongue may be seen in Figure 11b, page 49.

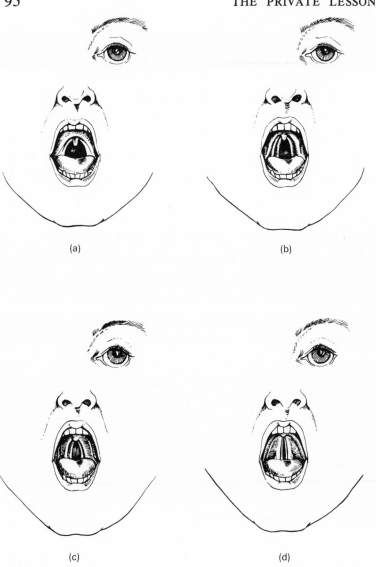

(a)   (b)

(c)   (d)

Fig. 17. Position of soft palate and uvula. **a.** CORRECT. Uvula long, pillars spread. Capacity distance to back wall of throat. **b.** FAIR. Space between pillars narrowed. Palate slightly higher than in **a. c.** POOR. Results in poor and nasal-sounding high tones. Note that uvula has practically disappeared. **d.** WRONG. Narrow space between pillars. Uvula out of sight. Palate closed; resulting tone is of falsetto quality.

PEDAGOGY DURING SECOND
AND SUBSEQUENT APPOINTMENTS

In the second appointment, after some casual con-
versation for the purpose of putting the pupil at ease,
ascertain what progress has been made by having her
demonstrate again the rolling motion with the Support
muscles. If she has failed to perfect this exercise take it
up again at this time and pursue it until satisfactory Support is achieved. Now return to the same vocal scheme
employed in the first appointment. However, since there
will be considerably more time for making sounds, take
care not to overwork the student. Involuntary muscles
behave unpredictably when they are tired. It is, neverthe-
less, very important to give these muscles all of the exercise that they can tolerate at this point. During successive weeks, they will become very much stronger. These
procedures should be repeated during at last three or four
appointments. Concentrate on extending the range upward in the upper zone and both ways in the lower zone.
From the very first appointment on, the student should
carry out these exercises with her eyes closed and holding
strictly to the "O" vowel. When she can do this with
complete confidence, student and teacher are ready for
another very important step.

Starting with the same C in the upper register and
holding the student's jaw (Fig. 16a), ask the pupil to
move her tongue back and forth very rapidly. The motion
is from the base of the tongue toward the front teeth and
back again. At the same time instruct her to alter her

vowel toward the "Aee." If this maneuver results in a far more ringing tone quality (while the tongue is moving in and out about six to ten times per second, and the jaw is held absolutely still) great progress has been made. Only about 40 percent of singers can make this tongue motion without moving the jaw. If the student falls within the 60 percent who cannot, have her practice without sound, preferably looking in a mirror. Sometimes the exercise is particularly difficult for the student, in other cases, the ability to move the tongue freely develops very quickly. It depends largely on overall vocal condition. When the pupil is able to execute the preceding exercise with the tongue moving (be sure the tongue is not fluttering as in a tremolo) on the vowels between "Aee" and "O," and the tone is a ringing one, ask her to follow the piano without stopping. With the tongue kept moving while she is sustaining the aforementioned vowel, move quickly up to an E-flat, which she will have heard as it was played thus:

Make the attack on the upper tone without stopping but let the student's tongue rest at ease. If this tone has a clear ring, another victory has been won.

Movement of the tongue without any action of the jaw is the next objective. Independent tongue action accomplishes more than one thing. First of all, it liberates the tongue from the swallowing muscles. The tongue is the front wall of the main vowel instrument, the pharynx (Figs. 10, 11, and 19a, pages 43, 49, 101), and therefore the tongue muscles that are involved in producing sound must be made maximally responsive. Nothing will accomplish this as quickly as the exercise involving controlled motion of the tongue. The vowels used here can lean toward an "Ee," an "Aee," or the "O" vowel in alternate turns. During the course of several lessons, have the pupil sing B, B-flat and C many hundreds of times until the tone rings beautifully.

If the tone rings while the tongue is in action but stops ringing when the tongue has stopped, it is evident that the proper tongue muscles have let go the instant the pupil has stopped the tongue movement. These same tongue muscles also influence the action of the soft palate and perhaps let it partly or completely close when the tongue stops moving. The tongue exercise must be continued until tongue coordination and strength has developed so that they will hold, even when the tongue is no longer in motion.

The exercise can be employed in many forms. One variation is to have the student use the tongue movement on the "Ee" sound on a beginning note, but with the tongue motionless on the succeeding note, on an "Aee" or an "Ee" vowel (do not go above an F-sharp or a G). It should be kept in mind that from G up the vowels of necessity become less pure because of decreased vowel format, fewer audible overtones, and less tongue control. Finally, the tongue exercise assists in developing the proper vowel formation.

All of these exercises should be done often. A. D. Clippenger, a famous teacher of voice, said: "The benefit derived from a vocal exercise comes with the continued practice of it multiplied hundreds of times after it goes well." By such means the mental patterns are strengthened and rooted deeply, and the muscles involved in the reflex actions become stronger and learn to coordinate more readily at each effort.

When the vowels have been formed and remain in the proper areas (which are the pharyngeal), the singer is ready to start vocalizing more than one pitch on the same breath. The succession of the steps that must be taken are very important. In leading the singer on several notes up and down the arpeggio on the same breath, caution is necessary in order to protect those good qualities which already exist. The only safe method is as follows: Establish correct vocal coordination with the proper tone quality on a pitch that the student can already perform and has performed many times from middle C and downward. *Memory of the new sounds the pupil is making becomes a great asset.* It is best to start with low B-flat or A. Start low and move up to D keeping the intensity level high; if the soft palate is open and the sound is strong, the vocal coordination will be correct. If the palate is closed both the sound and vocal coordination will be wrong. If the palate does not stay open, use the hum as in Figs. 18b and 19a. No one can hum with the palate closed. Make sure the hum is as in Fig. 19a, not 19b. After a number of tries, start on the B-flat, go up the triad to the third note, and back down. *It is important*

that the pupil always start with a sound that she under-
stands and can produce, that is, on the pitches she has al-
ready performed, C, B, B-flat, A and A-flat. If the pupil
should stop after the first pitch and make a readjustment
for the second pitch, it may be that she has lost the very

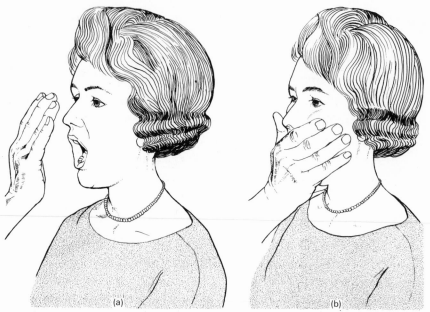

Fig. 18. This figure shows how to determine whether the soft palate
is open or closed.

thing the instructor is attempting to establish; namely, the
correct setting of the arytenoid cartilages with the use of
proper breath Support. When the sound is correct on the
tones from middle C downward, the larynx tension already
established will hold it between the two C's. The correct
sound is ultimately dependent on proper use of the nasal
resonator, i.e., dropping the soft palate (Figs. 19a and

20a). When the student is able to produce a beautiful
E-flat in the upper zone, a practical step is to establish
that pitch, move down to C, then A-flat, E-flat, C, and
finally A-flat. In other words, from the E-flat down the
arpeggio. If the student does not lose her Support on the

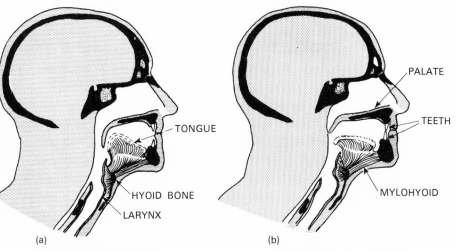

Fig. 19. Humming Positions. **a.** CORRECT. Teeth wide apart with lips
closed, tongue away from the back wall of the throat, the soft palate
dropped low. **b.** WRONG. An incorrect humming position. The palate is
closed, the tongue is in the wrong position, the jaw is tight.

way down, the lower tone will be very full as when practiced previously. However, there may be some detectable
weakness on the two middle pitches, A-flat and E-flat. If
these are strong, the pupil has already found some coordination.

The next step is to follow the same formula from the
upper E-flat. Move down fast and say "breathe!" When
the pupil has breathed quickly, have her move back up
again to the top E-flat. Although this is difficult, it can

be accomplished if the pupil has reestablished the same tone quality she had when she arrived at the A-flat coming down from the top. The tone quality will indicate

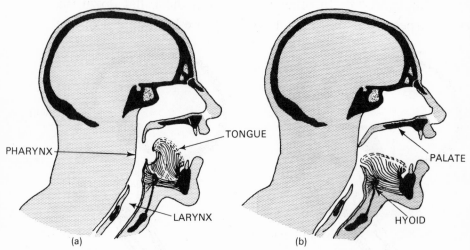

Fig. 20. Tongue Positions. **a.** CORRECT. The tongue in correct position with the mouth wide open and the soft palate down and away from the back wall of the throat. **b.** WRONG. Grooved tongue, too far back in the pharynx and the soft palate closed.

whether or not she has lost coordination in passing through the various notes on the way down, or on the way up. It is important that the proper vowels be employed in this exercise. It is always well to start with "Ee" or "Aee" vowels on the upper pitches and let them merge gradually into the "O" on the lower note and move back up until the last two notes above are either "Aee" or "Ee." This vowel procedure is especially useful because of the tongue and soft palate action required. On lower notes most singers will pull the larynx up on an "Aee" vowel, but they will leave it low and free on an "O" vowel.

On upper notes their tongues are often too low on the
"O" vowel, but will rise on the "Aee" and "Ee" vowels.
Although this is a temporary measure, it should be used as
often as necessary, i.e., any time the pupil appears to lose
correct coordination during the process of going through
many notes on one breath. There are many other helpful
procedures that could be mentioned; but for the experienced instructor they are not necessary. The important
tone quality at this point is that which is produced from
middle C to the C one octave above. For the female singer
who has sung incorrectly, this octave has always been the
"bottleneck." In fact, few singers of the past century have
sung this octave with acceptable quality. From this stage
forward, success with the female voice depends upon an
accurate assessment and understanding of the correct tone
quality in the octave between the two C's. It is not merely
carrying the pure lower quality clear up to the upper C,
nor is it a matter of carrying the upper C quality down
to the lower C. Either one of those two procedures by
itself would be painfully inadequate. What is definitely
required for good tone quality is incremental development
of the laryngopharyngeal resonator and the oropharyngeal
plus the nasopharyngeal resonators to the extent that they
carry the load about fifty-fifty at the F-sharp between the
two C's. (This is diagrammed in Fig. 13a, page 65.) It
is for this reason that recognition of tone quality assumes
such importance. Resonators for the "upper" and "lower"
must be open (soft palate down) and completely free of
interference,—a condition that is achieved when there is
proper Support. The resonators can then cooperate to set

the tone quality that must obtain for correct phonation throughout this octave. Only when this requirement is clearly understood will women singers arrive at their true potentials (Fig. 13a and c).

This discovery has been a fundamental breakthrough for the author. It has enabled him to develop good voices from ordinary material, and has never failed to improve on a voice when the principles have been rigorously followed. *However, slightly incorrect quality in this octave can throw off the whole plan of correct production.* The thing that will do it more quickly than anything else is permitting the student to form the vowels in the wrong areas of the vocal instrument. All vowels must be formed in the pharyngeal areas (Fig. 10, page 43). When tone production over this octave is mastered, the pupil will have no need for concern with high notes or low notes. In order for the octave between the two C's, and particularly the lower half (from C up to F) to be properly produced, Support must be so correct that all of the rest of the voice is inevitably good.

It has been the author's experience that it is not practical to vocalize scales, that is to say, consecutive notes in the diatonic scale, for at least six to eight months (and in some cases, longer). Because the singer is required to make a great change from her previous psychological approach to singing due to differences in tone quality and because the vowels are formed in a different area, the safe way to proceed is to choose a song with a wide range—from low A below middle C to about an F above the top of the staff. Have the pupil vocalize the song on the vowel that she presently can perform with confidence until there is a perfect vocal line going through the music. If the instructor wishes to experiment, he may let her sing the same song on the words without holding her jaw, and he will see how rapidly the sounds will change to something not so good. This is his clue to how he should proceed. He should not let her use the wrong sounds any longer than required to provide the example. It will soon be apparent that all the vowels must be formed the way the student vocalized: all basically behind the tongue. Only then will a good tone quality be obtained. Also, the consonants will begin to come correctly. At first these will be a problem because they are noises rather than vocal sounds. However, if the vocalization up to this point was correct, the pupil will have little trouble. The most practical way to make the transition from vocalization of the song to words is to let the student begin vocalizing, then whisper in her ear, "words" when she is well underway. In most cases this works out well, but she will lose the correct vocal sound if she places the vowel in the mouth. When the instructor is confronted with this problem, it is necessary for him to see that the student rehearses opening the soft palate and using the tongue exercise until she is able to keep the vowels in the pharynx where they belong. One of the most practical songs for this purpose is the tune from *Roberta*, "Smoke Gets in Your Eyes." This song covers the range from low G-sharp to upper F. It is an easy melody and most women can pick it up easily if they don't already know it. Choosing the first song is as important as the correct vocal exercise. The ability to sing one song correctly is very much like learning to ride a bicycle. If the student can ride one, she can ride them all.

PEDAGOGY FOR THE MALE VOICE

Training of the male voice is carried out in a manner very similar to training of the female voice. The main difference is in starting tones. As mentioned many times before, since the "bottleneck octave" is between the two C's in both sexes, it would seem logical that the two voices should be trained in exactly the same way. As the reader knows by now, the problem existing between the two C's is there, not because of vocal strength or the lack of it, but because of failure to make suitable resonating adjustments. All voices, whether male or female, bass or soprano, fall into the same category because the laryngeal structures and resonators of both the male and female are similar. For instance, the treble A which has 440 vibrations per second is between these two C's. It makes no difference whether a trumpet, a clarinet, or a human voice of either sex produces this pitch; it must be 440 vibrations per second. When this A is sung, the resonating cavities must be properly adjusted to control all of the overtones above the fundamental to properly resonate and reinforce this tone so as to give it ample quality, carrying power, and correct vowel partials.

Despite the logic of this concept, the reader may have noted that when a well-developed baritone sings A (440) the tone is ringing, powerful, and very heavy.

When the conventional contralto sings this same pitch, the quality is light and, compared to the baritone, very weak. This, however, does not prove the nature of the human instrument. It shows incorrect vocal adjustment (specifically, incorrect resonance adjustment) which does not permit necessary adjustments at the level of the larynx. For example, if the order is reversed, and a correctly developed contralto sings this same A (440) full voice, the tone will ring and will have tremendous carrying power, and also great quality. When the improperly trained baritone attempts to sing the same pitch, he may not make it at all or will go into what is termed falsetto. The timbre of the two voices may be vastly different, but the vocal mechanisms (from the standpoint of muscular orientation and the cavities that have to do with resonating adjustments) are anatomically and physiologically the same. Not understood in the past have been these facts: 1) The laws that govern the behavior of sound are the same regardless of the kind of instrument that produces a particular frequency. 2) The human vocal instrument is constructed according to a set pattern, and basically, all voices function in the same manner. Some singers and teachers have been led astray by the fact that the male voice is usually low by virtue of habit and training, and the female high for the same reasons.[30] Since habits have no bearing upon the capabilities of resonating adjustment in the human instrument (laryngeal adjustment follows quite normally if Support is correct), the "bottleneck octave" is always between the two C's in all voices, male and female.

However, because men have become used to singing

so much lower than women, it is important to find a comfortable pitch in a man's voice on which to begin the establishment of correct Support and vocal balance. Start him, therefore, with his lower tones approximately one octave below where one would start the female voice. B and B-flat one octave below middle C are very good pitches for this purpose. When these notes are firmly established with proper Support and resonance, encourage him to memorize the quality, sensation, and position as rapidly as possible. Here again, tone quality is the key factor.

In all male voices, from high C and through D-flat up to F, the tone quality, when correct, should sound like that of a well-developed contralto or heavy dramatic soprano on these very same pitches. As noted in Chapter 4, a sample of incorrect sound is demonstrated by Caruso on the D-flat above high-C on the Victor Red Seal record of Rossini's *Stabat Mater*. Although it demonstrates the remarkable throat condition and the Support behind this great singer's voice, it is not a legitimate sound. It is one that is produced by many otherwise outstanding female singers when their soft palates are closed. Such a sound is called falsetto. Although physically difficult at high pitches, a correct sound can only be produced if the soft palate is open so that the nasal resonators may be employed. On the other hand, it should be emphasized that the falsetto sound demonstrated by Mr. Caruso on this high D-flat is one that must be produced by the developing singer who is on his way to something better—that is to say, the great high tones that will be forthcoming when he learns to keep the soft palate open to the top of his range. The male voice has great difficulty finding proper larynx adjustment even at B-flat when resonance is incorrect (palate closed). However, when the palate is dropped so that an opening from the larynx into the nasal cavities exists, the sound is not only more in line with the rest of his voice, but the laryngeal adjustment occurs with so much more ease that pitches higher than C are within the reach of all tenors. Although it may not seem logical that the opening of the nasal resonator should facilitate laryngeal adjustment, the empirical observation has often been made in this studio that this is, indeed, the case. Over the "critical octave" it is practically impossible to achieve the incremental sharing of the laryngeal muscles for "upper" and "lower" unless the soft palate is lowered.

Experience has shown that nine out of ten tenors cannot make even the falsetto sound as produced by Caruso without a great amount of practice, training, and development of correct Support. Once the correct concept is established however, progress is very rapid.

If the condition is otherwise normal and Support is correct, proceed in this manner: sound the B-flat two octaves above. Hold the pupil's jaw, fingers along the cheek between the teeth to ascertain if the jaw is free (Fig. 15, page 89). If the larynx moves downward while the singer is inhaling and he is able to pull the abdominal muscles upward, as described, for the emission of sound, instruct him to make the same kind of a sound that the female would make in this part of her voice.[31] To him this would be the falsetto quality, but if correctly Supported, it will be very powerful like that of a dramatic soprano or a contralto *when her palate is closed* (Fig. 20b). Usually men cannot do this immediately because they do not know what is desired or required. When the teacher provides the example, they soon understand and if the prevailing conditions are right and damage has not been done previously, the singer will find the way to make the sound. This sound is now ready for development. The singer must learn to drop the soft palate to employ the nasal resonators (Fig. 20a). The humming exercise (Fig. 19) is employed as with the female singer. In some cases it is easier for a male voice to find the described tone quality at C or higher, but useful notes are usually somewhere between B-flat and high C. When this sound is basically correct, the intelligent singer usually comes very close to solving all the rest of his vocal problems.

When the soft palate is open on a strong, well-supported "falsetto," the quality resembles the legitimate male voice even though he remains on all "upper" as far as larynx adjustment is concerned. This step is very valuable because he now finds it easy to make laryngeal adjustments to bring in small portions of "lower."

From the foregoing it is apparent that the *difference in behavior of the larynx of male and female singers has come about by the incorrect belief that there should be a difference.* Proper coordination being established, the male singer can sing all the way up to high C with no more strain than the female has in singing these same pitches. Both the female and male larynx become malformed much as an individual's foot tries to adjust itself to a very pointed shoe.

One of the great difficulties arising through ancient misconceptions is the fact that widely recognized vocal critics have accepted as correct, the traditional, though faulty, sound in both the upper part of the male voice and the lower and middle part of a woman's voice so that the correct sound is often mistaken as being wrong. It simply does not resemble what they are used to hearing. This problem may persist for at least the next decade. Indeed, to say to many contemporary operatic conductors that nearly all male singers are straining their high notes would probably have the same effect as waving a red flag in front of a bull. The product of strain and overloading in the tenor's upper voice is accepted by nearly all concert and opera goers. Because the singer has to give his "very all" to make the note, it becomes that part of the tenor's voice which gives them the greatest thrill. A similar effect is achieved by the pole vaulter who, with a prodigious effort, vaults seventeen feet. Failure on the part of the singer to make this extreme physical effort gives the average audience the feeling that it has been cheated out of something. The young singer of today is, indeed, victim of distressing circumstances.

It should be emphasized that the type of singing described herein is *not* weak or puny. When perfect muscular balance is achieved in the tenor's larynx and when the sound is properly reinforced by the resonators, the tones are more beautiful than any words can describe, and the volume and carrying power is as great as that of any two tenors who sing with a strained larynx. Longevity of the voice is prolonged because there is no wear or tear.

Many young singers come to singing teachers with fairly correct coordination within the larynx itself. The natural potential of the human throat is awesome. In such cases trouble begins when the attempt is made to sing higher, louder, and lower without proper instruction. It is so easy to make trouble where there is none. For a young singer with a beautiful but undeveloped voice, it is most important to develop and strengthen all singing components (Support, larynx, and resonance) simultaneously, to retain the original beautiful quality. Emphasis of one factor over another will result in imbalance and the quality will be lost. When correct coordination is achieved, the more the singer sings, the greater his voice becomes. When the singer exercises the proper singing muscles vigorously, but never with throat strain, nature causes the voice to grow—as a rosebud develops into a rose.

CORRECT TONE QUALITY

It is difficult to put into words what is meant by correct tone quality. In the last ten years the author has been privileged to lecture to many hundreds of teachers to whom he was able to demonstrate the correct and the incorrect sounds with the living voice. These labors were fruitful. Where this demonstration was impossible, the information often did little good. In some cases it was actually harmful. Strange as it may seem, people who teach voice for many years only hear what they want to hear from a speaker, many times picking up a point or two and adding it to what they already are doing. This approach is worthless.

It is possible that 50 percent of the people who read this have never heard a correctly supported voice. This statement is not meant to cast a reflection on anyone more than on the author. He taught voice for many years before he was able to recognize when a singer was singing with completely correct Support. His generation was taught to believe that the numerous manifestations of strained tone qualities were merely different colors of sound or a particular singer's native quality. When the glottis is closed incorrectly an admixture of muscular entanglement occurs which impregnates the muscular structure of the larynx and makes it impossible for the singer to arrive at anything like his native quality. Efforts made to improve such sounds without going to the real source of the problem are like attempts to untie a knot by pulling the string tighter.

chapter seven
THE GROUP
APPROACH

The group approach is sometimes more effective than the private lesson. There are several reasons for this. First, the individual tends to be carried along by group psychology which can be controlled to advantage by the skillful teacher. Secondly, in a large group there are always some whose vocal condition and adaptability are very good. These individuals can be quickly spotted because of their superior tone quality and can be used as examples by the instructor.

FIRST GROUP MEETING

In the first meeting with a group, the instructor should take some time to describe the breathing muscles and how they perform for correct production of tone. Members of the group should go through breathing exercises together until everyone understands them and can use his abdominal muscles to raise up the entire abdomen, as described in the chapter on Support. The instructor should make a special effort to get each individual to apply the rolling motion. Secondly, each member of the group should be instructed to hold his jaws wide open with his finger and thumb along the cheek between the teeth so that he will notice if he bites with the jaw at the point of attack. Those who find that they do will now be aware that muscles of the jaw and tongue are undesirably tensed.

At his choir's first practice, the director may take an hour or more to explain the importance of Support by showing pictures and having individuals who employ proper Support demonstrate sounds. For subsequent rehearsals, individuals are encouraged to arrive an hour early, and during that interval they are taken, one at a time, to the piano, where they are moved through vocal exercises for two or three minutes. In this way it is possible to assist each individual, every other week, in a choir of fifty voices. As a result of individual attention, the group approach is more readily understood by all members, and in a relatively short time the tone of the choir has become quite "professional." From group vocalizing, based on individual work before choir rehearsal, the author has seen a large number of people develop fine solo voices who previously had never thought of singing a solo. In fact, many such singers feared at first that they were inadequate even for a choir. No matter how bad a choir may sound initially, the instructor can change the sound for the better in less than half an hour if the above mentioned starting procedure is used and the emphasis is placed properly, i.e., on the correct coordination of the muscles used for singing.

The following excerpts from a paper released within the last year by The American Academy of Teachers of Singing, emphasize the importance of good choral direction.

CHORAL SINGING
AND THE RESPONSIBILITY
OF THE CHORAL DIRECTOR

The American Academy of Teachers of Singing offers the following recommendations and advice on the subject of Choral Singing and the responsibility of Choral Directors for the vocal welfare of the members of their groups. It is a subject that is of vital importance to the young singers of our country.

During the last forty years choral singing has made great strides in American high schools, colleges, and universities. Likewise, church choirs, community choruses, and oratorio societies have shown a keener interest in the better type of choral literature and the improved performance thereof.

Commendable as this may be, it remains a fact that quality has not kept pace with quantity. The reason for this does not lie with the material at hand, but with the leadership. A director of a choral group, and this obviously includes the organist-director, may have many shortcomings or faults. He may lack leadership, musicianship, imagination, aggressiveness, or he may be an inept disciplinarian. Obviously he needs all these qualities but if he has no understanding of the human voice and its development, he lacks the most essential qualification for a successful choral director. Sir Henry Wood states clearly that he, not originally a vocal student himself, deemed it imperative to study voice and master its basic challenges before he would presume to conduct vocal performances.

It is wholly unreasonable to expect good tone, good blend, a free and natural emission of sound with respect to correctness of vowels, eloquent diction, and inspired expression from a group whose director is without an understanding of the functioning of the voice itself. The choral director is responsible for the tone quality of his choir. He must have the vocal knowledge to correct unmusical tone, faulty pitch, incorrect vowels, bad diction, and vocal straining. These do not, by some miracle, become beautiful by multiplication.

With the possible exception of professional groups, scrambling a choir into individual quartets is at best a questionable procedure. . . . The practice of having all voices within a section imitate any

one voice is likewise not conducive to good choral
tone. In the singing of *forte* passages this becomes
particularly noticeable. Natural, free emission of
tone by each individual need never be sacrificed
in order to achieve the desired result in choral singing. A student of singing should be encouraged to
participate in choral groups, but only if by doing so
he can, as an individual, enhance his vocal development, free from strain or tension. In such groups
where "imitation," the so-called "straight tone," or
other dubious methods are practiced, he has nothing
to gain and much to lose.

Only by proper vocal training can a singing
group ever hope to achieve even modest success.
This leaves no room in the field of choral directing
for those who have not had thorough and correct
vocal training themselves. . . .

Choral singing offers the opportunity of participation to more persons than any other form of art.
If and when the time comes that the directors of
choral groups will be men and women capable of
training and developing individual voices correctly,
(besides having the other necessary qualifications as
conductors) quality will more nearly keep pace with
quantity.

Robert Shaw and Roger Wagner, two eminent choral
directors in the United States, are personal friends of the
author. They are outstanding in their work, as evidenced
by their recordings, broadcasts and performances with
symphonies using large groups, because their natural
taste for good music has also endowed them with a taste
for good vocal sound. This has led to the selection of

singers who possess voices which are deep, full, resonant, and ringing. The author has heard Mr. Wagner say to a large group of sopranos, "I want you sopranos to sing as if you were mezzos; then you will get some 'body' to your voices!" A person endowed with such musical taste can detect interference in a voice quickly because this voice has a harsh sound and hence does not blend with other voices. But it must be remembered that these two men are very fortunate. They can select their singers from the best that Los Angeles, New York, and the rest of the nation has to offer. They also have the privilege of refusing those whose singing seems incorrect to them or those voices which they would not want in their ensemble. Their individual success serves as an excellent example of what singers with good tones can do for a choral conductor.

There are other choral directors in the United States who are popular, but whose choirs do not perform with such excellence. In some of these choirs the conductors are fully aware of what constitutes correct and incorrect voice production, but they elect to stick with thin, high, screechy sounds because these happen to meet their own particular taste. Regarding taste, everyone has, at one time, had an arbitrary tone quality in mind as being correct or beautiful. But when the correct sound has not only been discovered but also found to be integrated with what nature has intended, one should abandon the old and accept the new. He will eventually realize that the correct sound is much more beautiful and certainly much more practical.

Now, a few suggestions which, if followed, will serve

to protect the choral singer. This is, indeed, the instructor's first and most important obligation whether in school, church choir, or community chorus:

TENORS

First of all, in choral music consisting of four-, five-, six-, seven-, and eight-part harmony, the tenors carry the greatest burden. The tenors nearly always have to sing somewhere between the B below middle C and the A above middle C. Most of the time they sing between C and G in that octave. This is the "bottleneck" region of the voice (See Chapter 3). Until Support is correct, the throat free of interference, and resonance correct, it is impossible for any tenor to sing for even twenty minutes in that part of his voice without injuring his vocal mechanism. This is one of the reasons that most ensembles are suffering from a lack of good tenors. The tenor simply has to be better prepared than other singers. The author lavishes more attention on tenors than on the sum total of all of the rest of the singers in the choir. Incidentally, he has heard tenors whose voices blend fairly well into a group but who are unbearable when they sing solos. The reader has certainly noted this also. Of course, there are actually no such things as choral voices and solo voices. There is only one correct way to sing. If a singer acquires this technique, he is like an instrumentalist in a symphony. He plays his instrument in the same manner for a solo as he plays it in the ensemble. In both cases he is playing correctly. If there is a tenor section in the reader's choir that is potentially good, it can be made better by proper suggestion and therapy. First of all, tenors should be protected from difficult singing in rehearsal as much as possible. Since most choral tenors do not know how to sight read, they should be restrained from attempting notes that are completely beyond their vocal experience. Not knowing what the pitch is induces uncertainty, consequently they will sing incorrectly from a vocal standpoint. We have put this to the test many times. When rehearsing a choral number with many high notes, the tenors always sing these pitches with the voice production employed when they first found that pitch. They must not be allowed to make that first mistake. They can be protected if the accompanist plays the notes until they know the pitch and rhythm. Once they know the notes, they can concentrate on Support and correct voice production. In the meantime, they need this protection. A great choir requires a great tenor section. The only way to have that in a volunteer choir is to build each tenor's voice individually on the job, and it is not easy.

SOPRANOS

Sopranos must be protected in a similar way. However, the soprano is not as close to danger as the tenor because she sings most of her part in the "upper," away from the "bottleneck octave," and if she employs proper Support, she can improve as she performs, providing she keeps the vowels in the area where they belong (in the pharynx).

ALTOS

There is a saying about the altos: "Everyone who is not a soprano goes into the alto section." This usually makes a very poor alto section. The author often places young sopranos or even older ones, who have their lower tones underdeveloped, into the alto section for a whole semester, or sometimes for a whole season, for the purpose of developing the use of the muscles and resonators that must reinforce the tones in the lower range (Chapters 2 and 4). A good alto section can only be developed with time and concentrated attention on the "bottleneck octave."

Altos *MUST* especially learn to use the "lower" correctly as prescribed in the "Private Lesson" so that the quality between the C's is right. Harmony in a group depends largely on what the altos and the tenors do. If these two sections are wrong, i.e., if the tenors have a squeezed-up "lower" and the altos have a squeezed-down "upper" (fuzzy and weak), a praiseworthy ensemble is impossible. The late Father Finn of St. Paul's in New York has said, "The two center parts, the tenors and the contraltos, form the axis of your choral structure."

In group vocalization, breath support being well established, all of the women should be exercised in unison through two octaves from low A to high A. In many cases altos and sopranos can be interchanged to fill out and strengthen certain chords. A helpful hint for the singer in a choir is: "If I hear myself more plainly than the singer on either side of me, chances are that I am singing incorrectly."

BASSES

Many a bass singer makes the following mistake: sitting between two heavy bass voices, he attempts to hear himself better. He does this by pulling the larynx up against the hyoid bone, which causes the wrong muscles to tighten, thus carrying the sound more directly to the inner ear. This makes him think that he is contributing a large part of the sound. It may well be considerable sound, but it is usually very unpleasant and will not blend with the rest of the choir.

THE REHEARSAL

Before rehearsal the voices should be warmed up as a symphony orchestra warms up. Symphony players run fast scales and test their technique on difficult passages. Singers should activate their Support muscles, i.e., the breathing muscles. If these muscles are properly alerted, placed in position with buoyant and very definite upward Support, the singer, keeping the jaw and tongue free, can begin to make sounds, and in a few moments the resonating adjustments are likely to follow. In the author's choir, a number of exercises are employed, even including barking like a dog, a few times. When the choir sounds logy and drags during rehearsal, he re-awakens the singers both mentally and physically by having them do the things that are correct for vocal agility. When the choral number is taken up again, it sounds much improved.

Singers always begin to labor when alertness is replaced by indifference. This attitude is caused by a voice that is not mobile. The basis for this is a lack of reinforcement, *resonance*. A record player is worthless without a loudspeaker, loud or soft. The singer who tries to sing without proper resonance adjustment immediately starts a chain of bad reactions on the whole singing track. He is usually forcing the larynx to make more sound when, perhaps, it is already overloaded. When this occurs, hoarseness follows, and proper *resonance* is almost impossible.

Much can be learned about this from athletes. If the reader has been to a baseball game, he may have noted that the players were on the field several hours before the game, throwing the ball back and forth, running the field, and practicing at batting. When the pitcher warms up before the game, he begins by lobbing the ball, gradually he increases his power and speed, and by the time he has completed his warmup, he has done the equivalent of pitching four or five innings. A warmup is required for maximum efficiency and to avoid injury. The muscles that are essential for the pitcher must be alerted and, thus, pre-conditioned for the all-out effort.

In the choral warmup, the director should ask for singing without words in the beginning in order to give the singers the feel of the vocal sound. Words, involving as they do the consonants, are a severe handicap to the vocal warmup. After the singers have achieved proper

Support, a free throat, and resonance, they should vocalize the anthem without consonants until the sounds are right. The instructor can then say in the middle of an anthem— "words"—and they will start to sing the words better. Some will miss them, some will do them right. Those that are having problems should place their fingers along the cheeks between the teeth, as previously described, to determine if they are tightening the muscles of the jaw. Although the words of a few singers are not very plain, those who can form them clearly will make the chorus understood. If the words cause difficulty, omit them temporarily in rehearsal.

There is no longer any excuse for a choral conductor to say to himself, to his friends, or to his parishoners, "The members of our choir are not serious; they don't attend rehearsals well. When they do come, they don't sing well!" To the informed choral conductor, this is no longer a problem. As the singers find that they receive valuable vocal instruction, the seats are soon filled and before long there is a waiting list. Almost as a by-product, the choir sings beautiful music beautifully. The author has been criticized by some choral directors because he tends to separate the voice from the music. It is to be hoped that his critics can be made to see that where the symphony player walks into the rehearsal room with a perfectly built violin, the untrained singer has no such perfect instrument. His instrument must first be built and he must also be taught how to use it properly.

One of the most damaging mistakes made by the *a cappella* choirs of this country, particularly in the high schools, is to ask sight reading of those who really can't read a note. It would be difficult to arrive at a more rapid method of precipitating faulty vocal technique. The choral conductor who teaches music to a lusty piano accompaniment always produces a better tone quality from his singers although the actual performance may be sung *a cappella*. When the singer knows the music, he can release and sing with abandon. This is, of course, impossible if he has tightened his throat for weeks attempting to learn pitches and rhythm he could not read. The great damage is done in rehearsal, not in the performance.

THE HIGH SCHOOL CHOIR DIRECTOR

The choral conductor who has a real conviction on this subject is compelled to reason in the following manner:

> Since young people go to school to prepare themselves for the future, these students must be in better vocal condition after they have sung for him for four years than they were when they came in. If they are not, he has failed. He has not prepared them for the future. His chief job is to teach them correct vocal pedagogy to protect their voices so that by the time they go to college, they will be ready for greater, and more severe, singing based on the elements of correct voice production.

The choral director who takes a group of high school students and works them to the point where they can sing

an *a cappella* number whether they sing incorrectly or
not (perhaps to glorify himself as a conductor) is wrong-
ing these students. Teenagers cannot sing music that is
written for the mature professional singer. It should be
remembered that even professional singers have difficulty
with some of the things that high-school people are asked
to sing. The young voice cannot sound mature unless it is
especially endowed. These voices are few and can easily
be hurt by heavy choral singing at this age. The author
favors the following illustration of this point: A farmer
plants grain in the ground and all he sees at first is dirt. In
four weeks, if the moisture and the weather is right, the
emerging plant is dark green. If he did not know that it
takes an additional three-and-a-half months to become
tall, golden-yellow, ripe, and mature, he would be a farmer
that did not know his business. In the same way, it takes
time for nature to mature the voice. The choral director
should teach correct vocal principles, but he must bear in
mind that the high school pupil's voice will not, and
should not, become like that of the mature singer. Perhaps at the very best it can mature slightly. If the instructor bears these concepts in mind, the young voices in
his charge will grow up to maturity by the time the students reach their junior year in college.

It is the author's conviction that most high-school
music programs are improperly conceived. The proper
plan for high-school students in their first year above
junior high school is to teach them musicianship, sight
reading, and vocal principles for at least one year, based
on vocalization and including no singing of heavy choral

works. During the second year they can be exposed to light choral works. By the time they have reached the last year in high school, they are ready to perform effectively and safely. If the college choral directors (or the choir directors of those who do not go to college), would take these same young voices and continue the application of correct vocal principles, the nation would ultimately have a great crop of singers to fill all of the church choirs and community choruses; and in the process they would also have developed many great solo singers.

chapter eight
MISCELLANY

MUST A SINGER LOSE HIS VOICE WITH ADVANCING AGE?

The reader has perhaps wondered why so many great artists, who at one time enjoyed perfect voice production with unlimited range, quality, and control, lose their high tones at about the age of fifty. As in many other cases, scientific investigation provides the answer to this heretofore baffling question. There is actually one basic reason but two distinct manifestations. Consider first the case of the lower voices: baritones, basses, and altos. While the body is young, vital, and energetic, some singers find the correct Support and the correct coordination for the Support muscles quite by accident (which

is certainly a lot better than not finding it at all). However, if they really know what the elements of this wonderful coordination are, they can, if they wish, retain their
voices for the remainder of their lives, as some great singers do. When it is fully understood that correct Support
is provided by an upward thrust of those respiratory muscles which permit a person to exhale, and that exercising
the muscles in the abdominal wall which pull downward
negates this effect, the answer to the question posed above
becomes clear. Paradoxically, the factor which often pre-
cipitates voice failure is too much success, a situation
which leads to easy living, with too much rich food and
drink. Even without the burden of success, the human
body begins to change considerably around middle age,
particularly in the region just below the belt line. At the
age of forty-five to fifty, it is not unusual to find ten to
twenty-five pounds of additional weight in the abdominal
region. Also, with advancing age and concomitant lack
of exercise, the muscles in the body become weaker. Thus,
the aging baritone has twenty-five pounds more to lift
with only half of the strength to lift them. It is at this
point that the singer tends to substitute incorrect muscular
tension in the abdominal muscles for the correct upward
push toward the diaphragm. He confuses in his mind the
abdominal muscles that were once strong enough to lift
the substance of the abdomen straight upward and create correct Support with that other group of muscles which
pull downward (those which enable a mother to deliver
a child). The muscles in the lower part of the abdomen,

when vigorously exerted, release the Support which is holding the vocal folds together and, in addition, actually pull the larynx out of position so that it is no longer free to set the desired speed of vibration. Consequently, the singer starts to break on high tones. When this happens in a public performance two or three times, panic strikes, and the real trouble begins. Unless given immediate expert attention, it will lead to complete voice failure. It has been the author's good fortune to help a number of fine singers through this stage. When recognized in time, this vocal problem is actually one of the easiest to solve.

Trouble develops in a slightly different manner among tenors and sopranos (the *tessitura*). Strange as it may seem, it has been a common belief that singers with high voices can sing more easily if they "lighten" their tones. Indeed, this is the temporary illusion experienced by the singer who sings many high tones in a given performance. But after a decade of soft and weak voice production, a serious problem develops within the larynx itself. Sopranos who prefer to sing lighter on their high tones, are trapped into doing it for the same basic reasons as motivate baritones, basses, and altos aiming at high tones. They do not manifest proper Support. Later, when they have become older, fatter, and weaker, the excess weight in the lower part of the abdomen and the weakness of the muscles causes them merely to press instead of lifting up. This kind of pressure in the abdominal region forces the larynx against the hyoid bone and causes rigidity. There is no longer enough room for the arytenoid cartileges and the other components of the vocal cord action to behave as they were once capable of behaving. The high voices of tenors and sopranos which fade at this period of life exhibit symptoms of thin, shrill, strident sounds which crack very easily. In contrast, the baritones, basses, and altos exhibit very thick, overloaded sounds which seem to the listeners to be caused by using too much lower register or too much muscular action within the larynx itself. As stated earlier, the basic reason for voice failure in both groups is excess weight and weakness of the muscles employed for Support, but from the standpoint of tone quality, the symptoms are different.

The professional singer might well copy the foresighted man for whom a periodic check-up by a physician has become routine. "A stitch in time saves nine." The successful professional singer seems well advised to have frequent check-ups by a competent vocal specialist to avoid the troubles already mentioned here and many others. Recently this view was strongly corroborated by the following example. A lifelong friend of the author sang a song. The author knew this man when he was one of the outstanding tenors of the country, singing high C's, B's, and B-flats that were the envy of many other tenors. Now some years later, this singer was forced to struggle even at F, F-sharp and G. A mere shred of sound was displayed and it had a very unpleasant, unsatisfactory quality. If and when the author's friend reads these lines, he should recognize himself, and know that it is a sad, but true story. The worst part of this commentary is the fact that such tragedies happen constantly. Added to this misfortune is the plight of the vocal teacher who is in the same position as the physician. He cannot go up to a person and say, "You are in trouble, come to my office, and we will apply the cure." Quite often the contact is purely by chance. The author recently met one of his former pupils at a grocery store. During a brief discussion he said, "I must come to see you, I have a problem." Teacher and student immediately went to the studio to discuss the matter. His story was briefly this: A man with a family of seven children, he had been able to earn twenty-five to thirty thousand dollars a year for a period of some twenty-five years with his singing, and now he suddenly found his voice cracking at a G on two different takes on a tape in a very important studio in Hollywood. He was forty-nine years old and at least twenty-five pounds heavier across the abdomen than he had been in his youth. He could no longer raise the abdominal substance up against the diaphragm to give Support, but merely pressed and thus produced spasm of the larynx. Together, author and student rehearsed the fundamental abdominal rolling exercise for Support. In less than thirty minutes this singer was able to produce a high C that was actually better than any he had ever sung before. Afterwards he said, "Before tonight I was desperately trying to think of what I could do to get my children through college and supply the family's livelihood." That was over a year ago and the author told him then, "if you get in trouble, come running." He has not seen him since, so presumably all is well.

VOCAL DEFICIENCY

Someone has said, "Vocalizing is not the best method for overcoming vocal deficiency, understanding is better." We have all heard people say, "I wish I had a voice like—" and then they give a famous name, when, in reality, their own voices might be even better. The throat, like all the other parts of the anatomy, is standard equipment. One must be able to understand this equipment, and also learn how to manage it correctly in working to develop a great voice. What most singers do not understand is that the difference between their own voices and those of the famous singer they admire does not always lie in the native equipment, but often in the management of it. Of course, it must be understood here that no two voices are any more alike than any two faces are alike. Does this mean then that the author is saying *anyone* can become a great singer? The answer to this question, in brief, is: Whoever is endowed by nature with ample musical talent can learn to sing correctly if he is willing to pay the price. And what is the price? Certainly not money first. The price is simply physical control of the body by the mind.

HOARSENESS

Doctors agree that hoarseness does not necessarily imply a state of infection, but they have observed that quite frequently this and other voice changes can be due to unresolved emotional conflicts or fatigue. The larynx reacts to severe stress just as many other parts of the body do. Emotional problems tighten the vocal cords, and this tightening alters the volume and the pitch of their sound waves. Thus, the human voice continually reflects our various states of happiness, sorrow, worry, rage, and frustration. A joyful feeling permits the voice to ring. Grief may reduce it to a whisper. Constant rage and tension may cause the voice to become harsh and shrill. Guilt may make it thin. Total loss of voice has often occurred in a perfectly normal larynx that is paralyzed by acute anxiety. Some doctors believe that the throat should never be used as a musical instrument. It is our opinion that through proper vocal use, the larynx becomes the healthiest member of that part of the anatomy, thus it can fight off germs more readily than other less developed parts of the body.

SLIGHTLY ILL

Should the singer perform when he is slightly ill? Here again we can learn a very important lesson from the athletic world. The managers of professional athletes do not like to have them perform when they have even a slight cold. What is the singer to do? He has a concert scheduled, but he is not feeling well. "The show must go on" is a bad tradition. When such risks are taken, the results are usually very costly. The reasons can be deduced by common logic. The whole condition is abnormal. In order to compensate for the deficiency, the singer very often begins to employ incorrect vocal techniques.

Many voices have been ruined by just one concert. This does not mean that the voice will suddenly be gone. Singing under this abnormal condition starts incorrect coordination. It then reacts like the person who tells his first lie. He must immediately tell more to cover the one, and soon he is completely involved. The first reason a singer should not perform under such circumstances is that the people who have paid for their tickets are entitled to the singer's very best, not the product of a sick body and voice. The truth is that a sore throat is the most important alarm signal in the body. Many throat experts suggest that the best remedy for the sore throat victim is: stay in bed for forty-eight hours, consume generous portions of a high protein diet, drink plenty of fruit juices, stop smoking, and avoid talking as much as possible. When the body and the mind are well, the human instrument can perform gloriously. At this present writing, however, it is demonstrated by too few artists.

WHAT IS BEL CANTO?

Finally, the most baffling question of all. When a singer asks you, can you teach me the *bel canto method,* what in the world do you tell him? One dictionary of musical terms says the following: "The perfect (art of) song." By our mixed up ideas of singing, our young generation of singers are led to believe that *bel canto* is a singing system, a technique. Mostly they believe that it is a definite method. In Italian the adjective *bello* means "beautiful" and the noun *canto* means "singing." So we have "beautiful singing." What kind of a system is that? It is very difficult to explain to someone who has heard this term since childhood that he has been misled, and that this is not a method of singing at all. At the very best it is the result of a well-trained singer, at the peak of his ability, beautifully singing a beautiful song.

NOTES

1. Although Mr. Caruso is generally accepted as the greatest tenor of all time, his singing technique, placed under the microscope of present-day insight, reveals a few faults.
2. Floyd S. Muckey, *The Natural Method of Voice Production* (New York: Scribner's Sons, 1915), p. 128.
3. *Ibid.*
4. Miss Horne is the wife of the prominent young conductor of opera and symphony, Mr. Henry Lewis, who, over a period of six years, studied with the author.
5. Irwin Kellogg, *Why Breathe* (Los Angeles: Published by the author, 1927), pp. 6-7.
6. W. P. Bowen and H. A. Stone, *Applied Anatomy and Kinesiology* (Philadelphia: Lea & Feibiger, 1957), p. 307.
7. These suggestions are both unnecessary and usually harmful unless the soft palate is open. When the soft palate is closed (Fig. 18b, page 100), the singer makes an effort to get the vibration up and forward, but is unable to penetrate a closed door.
8. Wilmer T. Bartholomew, "The Role of Imagery in Voice Teaching and the Paradox in Voice Teaching," reprinted in pamphlet form from the 1935 *Proceedings of the Music Teachers National Association* by The National Association of Teachers of Singing (May 1951), p. 3.
9. A. Logan Turner, *Diseases of the Nose, Throat and Ear* (Baltimore: William Wood & Co., 1932), pp. 156-160.
10. Alexander Wood, *The Physics of Music* (4th ed., London: Methuen & Co. Ltd., 1947), p. 73. (Distributed by The Sherwood Press, Ohio.)
11. It is of interest that the early vocal scientists, because of lack of necessary measuring equipment (x-rays, etc.), were unable

to appreciate the large role played by the tongue and soft palate in the production of correct vowels.

12. Wood, *op. cit.,* pp. 23-24.
13. Douglas Stanley, *Your Voice* (New York: Pitman Publishing Corp., 1945), Fig. 11, p. 80.
14. Arnold Rose, *The Singer and the Voice* (London: Faber & Faber Ltd., 1962), Fig. 51, p. 198.
15. The tongue is misbehaving largely because the resonant cavities are out of adjustment due to a closed palate; the first mistake gives rise to the second.
16. The tongue exercise must not be confused with the fluttering tongue as in a bad tremolo. Reference is to a controlled tongue action, not a fluttering tongue.
17. Muckey, *op. cit.,* p. 145.
18. When the thyroid cartilage and the hyoid bone draw together at the point of phonation, it indicates that the cricoid-thyroid muscles are weak and need much development.
19. Stanley, *op. cit.* (Fig. 20), p. 98.
20. This phenomenon was touched upon by Dr. Stanley in some of his early writings, but perhaps because of lack of data, it was never developed. Stanley, *op. cit.,* p. 323.
21. Bartholomew, *op. cit.,* pp. 10, 12, 13.
22. Rose, *op. cit.,* p. 126.
23. An important clue to incorrect vocal production is noisy breathing at the end of a phrase. The singer should note that this is caused by interfering muscles. When the vocal cords are free to move, they open and close as quickly as one can blink his eyes. However, when interference is present, the interfering muscles must first be disengaged before opening can occur. This disengagement requires a fraction of a second during which time the diaphragm drops, drawing air through the only partially opened glottis. Hence, the noisy breath.
24. As heard on the Red Seal Victor record of Rossini's *Stabat Mater* on the D-flat above high C, in the aria "Cujus Animam" sung by Mr. Caruso. If Mr. Caruso had not closed the soft palate, the high D-flat in the cadenza would not have sounded

so much like a falsetto, or the conventional female sound. This has been demonstrated by many tenors.

25. The influence of the falsetto in the Russian school of singing for the male voice is clearly demonstrated by the power, control, and quality in the mature tenor voice, both in solo and ensemble, on the Angel Recording No. 36143 by The Red Army Ensemble.

26. The singer should never swim on the day that he sings. Water in the ears creates a strange resonating sensation which nearly always causes the singer to labor.

27. John C. Wilcox, *The Living Voice* (New York: Carl Fischer, Inc., 1935), p. 39.

28. *Loc. cit.*

29. Stanley, *op. cit.* (Fig. 20), p. 98.

30. Although the male voice tends naturally to deepen at puberty (due to an increase of the hormones testosterone and androsterone in the system and an increase in the thickness of the thyroid cartilage), if custom were otherwise, it could well be that the male would continue to speak in a higher voice.

31. Douglas Stanley and J. P. Maxfield, *The Voice* (New York: Pitman Publishing Co., 1933), p. 52.

INDEX

This book—and what it says—will be a light in the darkness for all individuals who are interested in the human voice as a sound-producing mechanism for both singing and speaking. This group includes singers, professional and amateur; teachers of singing, both private vocal teachers and classroom teachers in high schools and colleges; church choir directors; speech teachers who have encountered difficulty in getting the vocal mechanism to work properly; throat doctors; also public speakers or actors who suffer partial or complete loss of voice.

Joseph Klein is a successful vocal instructor, and with the aid of Dr. Ole Schjeide, a biologist-biophysicist, has filled the need for a book which clearly explains voice production—not in technical terminology, but in everyday language. Other books outline vocal facts. This book tells not only the "what," but also the all important "how."

This book is based on the premise that the human voice is a musical instrument which anyone with a good ear can learn to use skillfully—provided he, or she, is willing to devote the time and effort needed to learn how.

A focal point of their theory is "support" for singing and how to get it to work; they answer the question of registers in the human voice, discuss falsetto, and explain why so many singers have difficulty between *Middle C* and the *C* one octave above. Practical exercises are given that develop control of the tongue and the soft palate for proper vowel and resonance formation. There are chapters on private lesson pedagogy and the group approach.

The orientation of most vocal teachers is rarely methodical—their interest usually arises following a career of performance and although much information is available on voice production, most teachers and singers have little time or inclination to seek it out. This book provides

a complete, readable, and *workable* method. Its statements are securely based on anatomical and physical fact or on experimental data obtained from laboratories and studios throughout the world. It is a unique and valuable addition to our knowledge of the human voice.